Life History of Sultan Alimirah

Life History of Sultan Alimirah

Kadafo Hanfare

Sultan Alimirah was born in Awsa in a village called Furse in the late 1920s. The exact birth date is not known. His father, Hanfare Aydahis, was from the Aydahisso tribe, and his mother, Hawiomar, was from the Dambella tribe. Both of them were Afars from Awsa. Hanfare and Hawi had three children: Fatuma, Madina, and Alimirah.

The young Alimirah lost his father while his mother was pregnant with him. His father was killed by his uncle, Yayo, a powerful sultan, because of a political dispute among the family members. Later, while still a small child, Alimirah also lost his mother, who died of natural causes. He was brought up by his elder sister Fatuma.

Someone by the name of Halloh-Aydahis told this writer that he was sitting with Sultan Yayo on the night Alimirah was born. "We heard gunshots, and the sultan wanted to know why people were shouting. He was told that the widow of Hanfare Aydahis, Madame Hawi, had given birth to a baby boy. The sultan said, 'This boy will be the sultan of the Afar people.' We asked him, 'How come?' He told us, 'Look at the sky. Look where the stars are. That is why I am saying he will definitely become the sultan.'"

While Alimirah was still growing up, his older sister Fatuma married a very strong man in Awsa, Fitaurare Yayo Hamadu. Yayo Hamadu was the person closest to Sultan Mohamed. Sultan Mohamed trusted Yayo Hamadu and said of him, "His eyes are my eyes. His ears are my ears. His tongue is my tongue. Whoever obeys him obeys me, and whoever disobeys him disobeys me."

The full trust that Sultan Mohamed placed in Yayo Hamadu made him the most powerful person in Awsa and among the Afar people everywhere. By the time the young Alimirah reached twenty years of age, a fallout had occurred between the powerful Fitaurare Yayo and the more powerful Sultan Mohamed.

While Yayo Hamadu represented Sultan Mohamed, he performed major services for Ethiopia. One of those services was bringing tin from Assab port to Addis Ababa. At that time there were no cars or roads. The government of Addis had no way of reaching Assab. Fitaurare Yayo helped by bringing essential goods from Assab to Addis by loading the goods on camels.

During that process, Yayo met Tafari, the crown prince of Queen Zawditu at that time. Later Tafari became emperor and changed his name to Haile Sellossie, but the friendship endured. After few years, Italy invaded Ethiopia and occupied the country.

At that time, Emperor Haile Sellossie left the country. For the sake of keeping peace in his region, Sultan Mohamed made an agreement with the Italians. Part of the agreement was that the Italians would not interfere in his region's international affairs, and the sultan's people, the Afars, would not fight them. Later, Sultan Mohamed went to Rome to meet Mussolini. On that journey, Yayo Mohamed was with the sultan. At that time, Prince Emmiru, a cousin of Emperor Haile Sellossie, was in prison. The sultan and Yayo asked the Italians to allow them to visit Prince Ras Emmiru, and the Italians reluctantly allowed them to see Prince Ras Emmiru where he was being held. The sultan helped Prince Ras Emmiru financially and asked Mussolini to release him.

After the defeat of the Italians and the return of Emperor Haile Sellossie, things were different. Sultan Mohamed wanted the defeated Italian army to be left alone. He said that those Italians soldiers who were in the Afar region were allowed to stay in the area, and nobody was to fight them or harm them. If they wanted to leave, they would be allowed to leave in peace.

The sultan's order was not accepted by Yayo Hamadu. He insisted that, since the emperor was back, they should disarm the Italians, arrest them, and take them to Addis Ababa as the prisoners of war. Fitaurare Yayo himself told this writer that he disarmed many Italian soldiers and presented 999 of them to Emperor Haile Sellossie. While that action strengthened his friendship with the emperor, it ended Sultan Mohamed's trust in him.

The other point disputed between Fitaurare and the sultan involved the British, who wanted Awsa subjected under their mandate, as had been done in Eritrea. The sultan accepted. He even sent some young people, like his cousin Alwanyayo, to be trained in Assab. But Fitaurare Yayo Hamadu refused to accept this. He said, "Our emperor is back. The white people were defeated. Emperor Haile Sellossie is not the emperor for Ethiopia only, but he is the leader for all black people in the world, wherever they might be."

Those disagreements, together with other misunderstandings, brought a big disagreement between the two Afar leaders. Sultan Mohamed decided to fire Yayo Hamadu from his position, and in his place he appointed someone by the name of Assaiaytu. After doing that, the sultan called Yayo Hamadu to come to the village of Hamady Bary on a Thursday after the Zuhur prayer time. Yayo Hamadu told the sultan's messenger that he would be there by the appointed time, but he decided to leave the country altogether.

Fitaurare Yayo was a very clever man. He knew how the sultan operated and how he thought. He knew the sultan's mentality. He was very much aware why he had been called to Hamady Bury. He knew that it would be his last day on earth if he went there. Instead of going there, he communicated with Emperor Haile Sellossie. They agreed that Fitaurare Yayo should go to Addis Ababa. They also agreed on the timetable¾when he should leave and where the car should meet him.

After reaching that understanding, Fitaurare Yayo started preparing for departure. He told Alimirah, who was a young boy at that time, and other people whom he trusted that they would leave the area. They all agreed on the time to leave. The only person who knew about their exact departure time was his trusted wife Fatuma Hanfare, who happened to be Alimirah's older sister.

At that appointed time, they left. Fitaurare Yayo told his companions, "Once I was a lion in this land. I don't want to be less than that. *Ll lubak elle ekke kalol wakry makka.*" That was what he said in the Afar language. With them was a boy named Mady Bana, a servant for the young Alimirah. Mady Bana had decided not to go with them, but he was afraid to say so. He told them he wanted to urinate in the forest, and when they allowed him to go, he did not return. They went after him, and he told this writer that he saw them looking for him, but he hid himself in a cave in the forest.

After he made sure they were gone, he started running back to Aysaita. From Aysaita he went to Hamadibury, where the sultan was. There he told a guard that he wanted to see the sultan. The guard refused to let him in, asking what business he had with the sultan. The boy insisted that he had to see the sultan and tell him something important.

The guard went inside and told the sultan that there was a boy, Alimirah's servant, who said he had important news. The sultan said to let the boy come. Once inside, Mady Bana told the sultan that Fitaurare Yayo was gone and had taken Alimirah with him. He also told the sultan the identities of those who had left with him. The sultan ordered some of his guards to go after them and bring them back. But Fitaurare had already arranged for a car to meet him at Hadodasa in Mille. He escaped.

The sultan's guards went back and told the sultan what had happened. He said to let them go, that the cold weather of Addis Ababa and the bed bugs would take care of them. When they were tired of that, they would come back.

Meanwhile, two people had pursued Mady Bana when he ran away from Yayo and Alimirah, and these pursuers later told this writer that they'd meant to kill Mady Bana. These two people were Able and Alinaytu. Later, Mady Bana was forgiven for betraying Alimirah, and he lived and prospered in Aysaita. He was once again one of the people closest to Sultan Alimirah.

Anyway, Yayo Hamadu and the young Alimirah, together with their companions, arrived at Hadodasa in the town of Mille at the appointed time. There the cars sent by the Emperor Haile Sellossie were waiting for them. They escaped Sultan Mohamed's guards by boarding those cars.

After the sultan's guards returned home, Sultan Mohamed decided to send a delegation to Addis Ababa to take a message to Emperor Haile Sellossie. Sultan Mohamed picked Asiyaytu as the head of the delegation, and he also told Abadirta to join the delegation. Mr. Asiyaytu was given a letter from the sultan to deliver to the emperor. In that letter, Sultan Mohamed explained his health situation and said that if he had not been sick he would have to come to Addis Ababa to explain everything himself. He also explained about Yayo Hamadu and the young Alimirah. He said that Fitaurare Yayo had been one of his trusted people but had, for some reason that was not clear to him, betrayed him. The sultan asked that his majesty, the emperor, send Fitaurare Yayo back to him, along with the sultan's young nephew Alimirah. Sultan Mohamed had told Asiyaytu to take with him some gold, money, butter, and other important items to bribe the emperor's officials to send Yayo back.

Mr. Asiyaytu was not an educated man. He was not equal to Yayo Hamadu, even though the sultan had appointed him to replace Yayo Hamadu. But Mr. Abadirta was a somewhat learned man. He could read and write. When they arrived at Addis Ababa, instead of delivering the message to the emperor, they gave Yayo Hamadu everything they had brought from Sultan Mohamed. Although Asiyaytu was not aware of it, Abadirta was already allied with Yayo. Fitaurare Yayo took everything¾the gold, the butter, and other goods sent by the sultan¾and distributed them to the officials as a gift to them from himself.

The message has not been delivered to the emperor, but Asiyaytu and Abadirta returned to the sultan. Asiyaytu unknowingly lied to the sultan. He thought that, even though he had not met the emperor personally, Abadirta had delivered the message by giving it to someone who would pass it to the emperor. Abadirta has already betrayed the sultan by allying himself with Yayo Hamadu. When the two men returned together, they lied to the sultan, saying that everything in Addis Ababa was okay. In Afar language, they said, *"Allie bagi warkat enna lie,"* meaning, "the highlander's heart for you is *as whale as apoper."* In Addis Ababa, that means "everything is okay."

But everything was *not* okay. After six months in Addis, Yayo Hamadu and the young Alimirah were called to see Emperor Haile Sellossie. The emperor renewed the title of *Fitawrare* to Yayo Hamadu and gave the title of *Dejazmach* to Alimirah. He also gave them well-trained army soldiers to go with them to oust Sultan Mohamed.

In those days, there was no modern communication. Therefore, Sultan Mohamed and his people had no way of knowing about the invasion that was going to happen. The invading army's tactic was to take many empty trucks with them. Whenever they found an Afar person on the road, they kidnapped him, put him on a truck, and took him with them, so as to keep the invasion secret. They were successful in that until they reached the town of Sardo. Sardo was sixty kilometers from Aysaita, the sultan's capital. The invading army led by the general and Fitaurare Yayo Hamadu left Sardo at night to go to Aysaita. To keep from being detected, they kept the vehicles' lights off.

The children of the sultan lived over the top of Gargory Hill. From the top of Gargory Hill, Kadda Yayo, the oldest son of the sultan, saw the army's movement. When he saw the cars moving without the lights on at night, he figured that it was an invasion. He ran toward Hennale, where his father was staying. There he found his father sleeping. Kadda Yayo woke him up and told him what he had seen. The sultan told his son to go back. He could not believe that anybody would invade him, and certainly not because of Yayo Hamadu.

Kadda Yayo went back to Gargory Hill again and clearly saw what was going on. There were hundreds of trucks carrying an army of soldiers. He was sure it was an invasion. He returned to his father and told him that they had to defend themselves. They had to call their guards, their soldiers, their people¾everyone. It was an invasion, coming to overthrow the sultan.

The sultan told him to calm down. Nobody was coming to overthrow him. Haile Sellossie wouldn't do that.

Kadda Yayo told the sultan's guards to be ready to defend their sultan. When the sultan heard that Kadda Yayo was ordering people to defend him without his permission, he called him to him and said, "If you are that much afraid, come and sleep under my bed, but don't tell anyone to defend me. There is nothing to defend, because there is no invasion."

Kadda Yayo was angry. He went back to Gargory. From there he saw the invading army entering Aysaita. Aysaita was about four kilometers from Hennale, where the sultan was staying.

The invading army stayed in Aysaita overnight. Early in the morning, the general who led the invading army with Fitaurare Yayo woke up to go to Hennale. Before they left, the general looked at Hennale through a telescope. He saw a lot of Afar people gathering around the palace, which they called Gasso. Those people, especially the young Afar people, were armed to the teeth. The general was surprised to see that. He called for Yayo Hamadu and said that Yayo had told him that there were no people around the sultan, that nobody was going to fight them. But now, there were all these people.

Fitaurare Yayo told the general, "I never said there were no people. I know there are people around the sultan. I also know those people are armed. I know they are very brave people who love their sultan and will defend him to the death, but to do that, they need a leader who can lead them, someone who can give them orders. That leader is me, and I am with you. So don't worry. No fighting. I promise."

Fitaurare Yayo took the army to Hennale Gasso. There they found the sultan Mohamed sick in bed. As Fitaurare had promised, there was no fighting. When they took the sultan, his wife Madina killed an officer who had captured him, and she was killed right there. Another man killed another officer, the guard killed another, and a cow killed another. That was all. All the other Afars were just looking around when the sultan was taken away to Aysaita.

When they arrived at Aysaita, the sultan wanted to know what was going on. They told him he had been ousted from power by order of the emperor Haile Sellossie and had been replaced by the young Alimirah, who happened to be his nephew. The sultan thought the fools had appointed Yayo Hamadu in his place, but if it was to be Alimirah, that was okay, because he felt that the power would still remain in his hand. He also said, "I don't want to see Yayo Hamadu, but I want to see the young Alimirah, so please call him. I want to see him."

The young Alimirah came. Sultan Mohamed told him, "I congratulate you. You have as much right to be the sultan of Awsa as I do. I have *no* problem if you succeed me, but I want to give you some advice. I know that my father, Sultan Yayo, killed your father Hanfare, who was his nephew. It was a family dispute. I myself do not agree with that kind of political killing. That is why, in my twelve years in power, I have not killed any of my relatives. Let us forget the past. What I am telling you is this: Don't kill my children. For that matter, don't kill any of your relatives."

The young sultan Alimirah promised him that he would not do such a thing. Later on, after having coffee together, Sultan Mohamed was taken by the victorious army to Addis Ababa, and the young sultan Alimirah remained in Aysaita. After the old sultan was gone, Yayo Hamadu called for a public meeting. At that meeting, they informed that people that Alimirah was Amoyta, and Fitaurare Yayo would be representing him in all matters.

To inform everybody in the country, they formed a committee. The committee chairman was a person named Kurba. Representatives went to every corner of the country, repeating the same message: "Alimirah is the new Amoyta. He is the son of Hanfare Aydahis. He is a great-grandson of Mohamed Hanfare on Ellolta. Fitaurare Yayo Hamadu¾whom you all know as an experienced, great leader¾will assist the young Amoyta in administrating the country and act as his representative."

Meanwhile, Sultan Mohamed's children left Gargory Hill and went to Hennale palace. They were led by Kadda Yayo, the oldest son of the sultan. At Hennale, everybody gathered. Some of them were armed, and some were not armed, but they were all ready to fight the invaders. Kadda Yayo and his brothers decided to leave Hennale for the Handag area. Everybody followed them, wanting the brothers to lead them in resisting the invasion. Kadda Yayo and his brothers decided against resisting.

They wanted to explain their situation to Emperor Haile Sellossie in Addis Ababa. They wanted to follow their father.

To do that, only the older male children went to Addis Ababa. They were: Kadda Yayo, Kadda Alimirah, Kadda Allo, Kadda Aydahis, and Kadda Hanfare. (The word *kadda* means "older.") Their decision to go to Addis Ababa rather than fight was top-secret at the time, because angry males could not do anything.

Therefore, they decided to escape their enemies as well as their friends. To do that, they put together a plan. They called for a man named Ado Hamadu, a famous magician from a Socabla tribe, to do escape magic for them. "It was daytime, but after the magic, the place looked so dark that only those who escaped with Yayo and his brothers could see each other. The others they did not see anything." Kadda Yayo and his brothers and their friends escaped Handag. They went back to Gargory. From there they walked all the way to Bati, about 300 kilometers.

At Bati, the central government representative found out who they were. He captured them, put them in a car, and took them to Addis Ababa. There he told the emperor that he had arrested them in a fight. Their followers were defeated, and he captured them and put them all in prison. After a year in prison, the brothers and their followers were pardoned by the emperor, but their movement was restricted to Addis Ababa. Later on, they were only ordered not to go to Awsa.

Sultan Alimirah ruled Awsa from 1947 until 1975, when he was invaded by the Derg army in an attempt to kill him. He left Awsa at that time and established an organization called ALF (Afar Liberation Front) in order to oust the Derg and Magistu from power in Addis Ababa. In those days, Sultan Alimirah lived in exile in Saudi Arabia. After twelve years of fighting, the sultan returned to Ethiopia. The Derg and Mangistu were defeated. Sultan Alimirah died in May 2011 in Addis Ababa from old age and natural causes. He was about ninety-three.

Because I grew up in Gasso, the palace, I want to write about some important events that took place. The first event is one I don't remember, but I heard about it from everyone who was there at the time. That event was about someone called Sahle. In those days, it took months to go from Awsa to Addis Ababa. When the sultan and his assistant Fitaurare Yayo Hamadu were on that journey, the governor of Bati sent someone named Sahle to look after the day-to-day affairs of the people in the area until their leaders returned. However, Sahle did not see himself as a caretaker but as a real power and the leader of the area. In that situation, he got support from the former sultan's supporters and from those people who saw Yayo Hamadu as their enemy.

Those people considered Sahle to be their leader and started making songs to praise him. Some of those songs in Biritic said, "*Sahle yanimbarah maha abeyo mayou.*" In the Afar language, the translation was, "As long as Sahle is around, I do not worry about how I can help my son."

The afar people in Awsa were divided. One camp supported Sultan Alimirah, while the other camp supported Sahle. There was a lot of tension and fear of civil war in Awsa. When Emperor Haile Sellossie heard about that, he immediately ordered Sultan Alimirah and Fitaurare Yayo to go back to Awsa. He also ordered Sahle to leave Awsa and go back to Bati.

Sahle said good-bye and left Awsa. On his way, his car stopped. He and his driver wanted somebody to help them push the car to get it started, but nobody wanted to help him. Those people who had been his supporters, who had been singing his praises, would have nothing to do with him in his time of need. He walked all the way back to Aysaita and begged the sultan to tell some people to help him push the car. The sultan ordered some of his guards to go and help Sahle. After the car started, Sahle left, but he told the people, "You Afars in Awsa are opportunistic people. If I were Sultan Alimirah, I wouldn't depend on you." The people told him to leave and not to worry about them or their sultan. That was how the Sahle situation ended.

After Sahle was gone, the sultan started focusing on development. He opened modern schools and built more traditional Kuranic schools, Arabic Madressa. He also built some clinics. People started farming. Cotton was introduced as a cash crop. Maize and other crops were also expanded. In building schools, he got help from a European named Mr. Marry from Norway. Together, with the help of Emperor Haile Sellossie, they built elementary school in Aysaita.

Sultan Alimirah and the Norwegian named one school Mohamed Hanfare, after one of the modern sultanate's founders. The Ministry of Education at that time named the school Atie Gabemaskal, after one of the Ethiopian kings. After the downfall of the Derg, that school got its original name back. It was called Mohamed Hanfare School.

The sultan also got help from Mr. George Savard, who lived among the Afar people in Awsa in the sixties. He was a Canadian from Guibee. He built a library in Aysaita. He also built a small school in the Kaloptale area, where he himself lived. He was loved by the Awsa people, but he had to leave that area when the Derg came to power.

Before that, in the early sixties, one of the late sultan's brothers, Omda Mohamed, revolted against Sultan Alimirah, and went to Doka. He camped at the place called Teru in Doka. There, a lot of people joined him. He trained them and prepared them for invasion. Teru is probably 300 kilometers from Aysaita, but those there were no cars on the roads. After six months of preparation, it was time to invade and attack the sultan's forces. Omda Mohamed had about five thousand supporters with him¾armed and unarmed. A person named Fatumah-Aydahis¾or Aysahishassan Dimu¾was a leader of Omda Mohamed's supporters.

Sultan Alimirah's supporters were led by a fellow named Salih Almirah. The sultan's supporters were very few, but they were supporting legitimacy. People like Fitaurare Yayo Hamadu, Alwan Yayo, Always Mohamed, Ebly, Alimaytu, and all the important people were with the sultan. When Fitaurare Yayo saw that their supporters were few in number, he contacted Emperor Haibe Sellossie and told him what was going on.

The emperor asked how can could interfere between an uncle and a nephew's dispute. What he *could* do was to send wise men to reconcile them. When Fitaurare found out that there was no military help coming from the emperor, he went to Bati and invited the governor of Bati at that time to place the militia under him. Without the knowledge of the central government, the governor ordered two thousand militia soldiers to go to Awsa and help the sultan's supporters. Fitaurare Yayo put the militia force in the city of Aysaita and hid them from the public.

At that time, Sultan Alimirah was in Hayu, where he had a summer house. This writer was with the sultan at Hayu. One day, early in the morning, everybody was called to the sultan. When they came, he told some people to board one of his two cars. I was one of those travelers who boarded the sultan's car. When the sultan came out to enter his car, he could not see some of his closest bodyguards.

He was furious. He asked about them by name, but nobody knew where they were. So the sultan said we should go. The sultan's driver, Hassan Yamane, said, "Why we don't wait for them? They will come." But the sultan said no, so we left. We found four or five of the bodyguards standing along the road, waiting for our car to arrive. The driver stopped the car, and the sultan ordered the men to get into the car¾except for two of them: Omer Mohamed and Hassan Aydahis.

The sultan told them, "This position I am holding now is given to me by Allah, and only Allah can take it from me. You people think that, because of the war situation, I need you more now than before. You are wrong. I depend only on Allah. You, Omer Mohamed, leave your gun here with us. Go from here, because you belong to the Aysi tribe. You will find your Aysi tribe on those mountains. And you, Hassan Aydahis, your tribe is from Elawly Dambella, and they are also over those mountains. Go join them. I don't need you."

One passenger in the car, a cousin of the sultan called Allohanfare, begged the sultan to forgive the men. The sultan accepted the request and forgave them. They got back their weapons and were told to board the car. Only Omer Mohamed accepted the offer to board; Hassan Aydahis refused. We left him there.

On the same night, Omda Mohamed's forces started attacking. They were far from Aysaita. We saw the bullets' light, but we could not hear the sound. But we knew the attack had started.

Many of Sultan Alimirah's forces, led by the powerful Yayo Hamadu, rushed to the front to stop the attackers where they were. They did not want them to advance to Aysaita. But Omda Mohamed's forces were strong. They defeated the sultan's forces at the place called 3 Gasso. They killed someone who looked like Yayo Hamadu, and they were very happy. But Yayo was alive and well. As a last resort, if the invaders tried to enter, Yayo was ready to use the foreign militia he had hired from Bati. He himself returned to Aysaita.

As I said before, I was at Gasso, the palace of Aysaita. The sultan was there. He was armed, but he was also praying. His guards tried to evacuate him from the palace, but he refused to leave. He said he was ready to die right there. His older sister, Fatuma Hanfare, was also there in the palace with him. A person named Saleh Alimirah was the leader of the palace guard. I heard him giving orders. Once, late at night, some guards brought in a wounded man named Massikoh Gaas. The man was badly wounded.

There was a traditional Afar doctor to attend to the wounded at the palace. The wounded man told the guards and the doctor that they should keep the wounded away in hiding. You can treat them, but don't let them see anybody. I also heard him giving an order to an armed guard: "Your job is to defend the area of the school." The guard asked him, "Alone?" "Yes," he said, "alone. *You* know you are alone, but *they* don't. Hide yourself in the forest and keep shooting."

Fortunately for the sultan, the victorious army of Omda Mohamed did not enter Aysaita. Instead, they surrounded Aysaita and crossed the Awash River to Dora in Afar at the Abrobaryh Fagi crossing. After they crossed the river, they settled in at Ellalty Hanfarehgayra. There they made themselves sitting ducks. Had they proceeded instead to Aysaita, it is the opinion of this writer that they would have succeeded in driving the sultan out of the palace and maybe from power altogether. But instead of entering Aysaita, the capital of the sultanate, they passed behind Aysaita and crossed the river.

They camped on the other side of the river, and there they waited, with nothing to do but celebrate their victory. The sultan and the powerful Yayo Hamadu regrouped their followers and gave them food, water, and a pep talk to encourage them. Then, together with the Bati militia that was hiding in Aysaita, they crossed the river at the same place their enemy had crossed¾Abrobarihfagy. Then they started attacking. The Omda Mohamed forces tried to resist, but the power balance had shifted.

Yayo Hamadu led the sultan's forces, and they could not be resisted. A lot of people died on Omda Mohamed's side. How many people died, we do not know, but this writer heard as a child that someone named Abile from the sultan's side shot more than forty bullets at Omda Mohamed's forces. None of the forty bullets missed the target. That shows that a lot of people died.

After losing so many people, Omda Mohamed's forces were defeated. They started surrendering by waving white cloths. The first to surrender was a fellow named Fatumah Aydahis or Aydahis Hassan Dimu. When he surrendered, some people who had lost their brothers, relatives, and friends tried to kill him¾especially the Maandita tribe, because Fitaurare Yayo Hamadu's nephew, his brother's son Yayo Hayou, had been killed by Omda Mohamed's forces. But Fatumah Aydahis had relatives among the victorious forces, and they protected him. Later on, the remaining fighters also surrendered.

Omda Mohamed and a few fighters hid in the forest and continued fighting until two people showed up waving a white cloths to surrender. They were Egahle and Yayo Barule. Those two people gave themselves up and told the attacking fighters that Omda Mohamed was wounded and bleeding. They said, "If you continue attacking he might die. If you want to capture him alive, let us go and bring him to you. For our guarantee, both of us will surrender our weapons."

The attackers thought this was a good idea. After taking all of their weapons, they let the two men go. The fighters stopped attacking and waited for the men for about half an hour. When they did not return with Omda Mohamed as they had promised, the sultan's forces grew suspicious. Their suspicion was correct. Everything the two men had said about Omda Mohamed had been a lie.

Instead of bringing Omda Mohamed, they had run away with him. When Fitaurare Yayo Hamadu heard what had happened, he pressured the fleeing men with forces, but Omda Mohamed and a few of his close friends escaped them. They went to Djibouti, where the French were at that time. The French soldiers tried to disarm Omda Mohamed and his followers, but Omda Mohamed refused to disarm. So the French told them they could not enter Djibouti.

The fugitives instead went to Enter, and from there they crossed to the Tigray province. From Tigray they went to Biru, where they met the Afar chieftain called Mohamed Ahaw. Mohamed Ahaw welcomed Omda Mohamed and his remaining followers. By the way, some of Omda Mohamed's followers died on their way for lack of water. After Mohamed Ahaw welcomed them, he thought that he could not hide Omda Mohamed from the powerful sultan Alimirah, so he took him to Addis Ababa. In Addis, the central government put Omda Mohamed in prison.

In 1963, when this writer came to Addis Ababa as a grade one student at Dajazmach Wonderad School along with other Afar students from Awsa, I met Omda Mohamed in prison. That was the first and last time I saw Omda Mohamed, even though I am related to him. He and my mother are first cousins. One of Omda Mohamed's followers was someone I looked up to as a child. His name was Aysahis Ahmed or Arbaoyta, and he was somewhat educated. During the conflict, he had been an accountant for Omda Mohamed. When Omda Mohamed's fighters were defeated, he said that they had two camel loads of money.

Omda Mohamed told him to throw that money into the river. Arbaoyta told Omda Mohamed, "You are fighting your nephew to take power for yourself, but as for me, my struggle is for money. How come you tell me to throw this much money into the river?" Omda Mohamed was serious. He pointed his gun at Arbaoyta and ordered him to throw all the sacks of money into the river, which he did reluctantly.

When he told this story, he made a lot of people laugh. Omda Mohamed was pardoned by Emperor Haile Sellossie and was released from prison. but he could not go to Awsa. When the Dung came to power in 1974, he went to Awsa. In later years, I heard that he had gotten sick and died in Baadu.

In Ethiopia, a King Ends His Exile:

Afar Sultan Insists on the Right of His People in Both Eritrea and Ethiopia to Vote on Uniting

Dubti, Ethiopia

The man who would be king is finally home. He has returned to his native region after seventeen years of forced exile as an opponent of the previous Ethiopian government. Amid hand-kissing, shouting, and singing, Sultan Alimirah arrived recently in this small northeastern town, deep inside the impoverished territory of his people¾the Afars, who have a reputation as fierce fighters and who want to be united. His success in handling the problem of poverty and the question of unity will in part determine whether Ethiopia will be able to maintain peace, not only within its borders, but with its newly self-proclaimed independent neighbor: Eritrea.

Eritrea is the northern Ethiopian province that fought for thirty years to win the right to a referendum on staying with Ethiopia or choosing independence. A vote is planned within two years. But the Afars, who are divided between Ethiopia and Eritrea as well as the neighboring country of Djibouti, want their own referendum on the question of unity. And that's the sticky point for Ethiopia¾and Eritrea. The Afars want the right to unite under one ruler, the sultan, in Ethiopia. They claim parts of several provinces in Ethiopia and a critical part of Eritrea¾along the coast from just south of the port of Massawa down to and including the other port, Assab.

Eritrean rebel leader Isaias Aferworki says that the Afars in Eritrea cannot secede from Eritrea to join an autonomous Afar region in Ethiopia. Mr. Aferworki strongly opposes the loss of any land¾hard-won in the Eritrean struggle for self-determination¾to Ethiopia. Afars can unite within Eritrean borders, he says. But at a political conference in Addis Ababa in July, the soft-spoken, dark-skinned sultan, whose short, white beard matches the color of the long robe and Muslim skull cap he usually wears in public, took the floor. He insisted on the right of his people in both Eritrea and Ethiopia to vote on uniting within Ethiopia. Monitored interviews with top Afar leaders in Addis Ababa and during the sultan's four-day ride home in a convoy of Land Rovers guarded by Afar fighters in Toyota pickups, indicate they do not want trouble with Eritrea. But they absolutely insist on the right of their people to decide their own future.

"We are not against Eritrean self-determination," says Ahmed Alimirah, a son of the sultan and head of the military wing of the rebel Afar Liberation Front (ALF). "We'd also like the Afars to have the right to self-determination. We are going to govern our affairs, rule our area, and we'll have an autonomous Afar region in the Afar area. The Afar people [in Eritrea] will decide whether they [would] like to join the Afars in the rest of Ethiopia or want to remain within Eritrea."

And if the Afars in Eritrea vote to unite with their brothers and sisters in Ethiopia proper but are denied the right by the EPLF, will the Afars fight? Ahmed declines to answer directly. But he notes that the ALF helped fight the army of now-deposed Ethiopian leader Mengistu Haile Mariam, once

11

considered one of the biggest and best-equipped in Africa. Another Afar political leader suggests that Eritrea, Ethiopia, and Djibouti could solve the dilemma by allowing the Afars unrestricted travel across the boundaries. They might then technically still be residents of one of those three states but feel united under the sultan's rule. Other Afars were not certain this would be acceptable.

Meanwhile, the sultan faces a host of complaints from his people about their loss to the government of key grazing and croplands along the fertile Awash River, a lifeline in their dry region. "We came to complain about losing our lands, our rivers," says Abdu Adu, an Afar clan leader who greeted the sultan at one of his stops on the way home. "We cannot feed our children. And we cannot teach our children where there are no schools."

Sultan Alimirah also promises schools, health clinics, and foreign aid to the Afars. "We ask the world community to assist us until we get into shape." He says he had a hard time recognizing some of his old colleagues here because of the thinness of their faces and their tattered clothing. But his first priority is religion. He wants to impose *sharia*, or Islamic law, among the Afars, a Muslim people.

"I'm very happy to be back after seventeen years," he says. "First of all I want to restore the morale of the people. The Mengistu government introduced strange customs [drugs, alcohol, and stealing, he later alleges]. We'll try to go back to our Islamic and good traditions. After that we'll concentrate on the economy, which Mengistu destroyed." The rights of non-Muslim Afars will be respected, he says, adding that even under his Islamic rule, women will have the right to university educations¾but the sexes will be separated after primary school. He also promises his people to try to settle peacefully the long, traditional grazing-land and cattle-raiding disputes between the Afars and the similarly well-armed neighboring Issa tribe.

In Memory of Ethiopian Patriot, Sultan Alimirah

EthiopianReview.com | May 11, 2011
by Ambassador Kadafo Mohamed Hanfare

Sultan Alimirah Hanfare (1921-2011) was born in Awsa, Ethiopia, in a village called Fursee. He was born to father, Hanfare Aydahis, and mother, Hawy Omar, in the early 1920s. His grandfather, Mohammed Hanfare Illalta, was a famous king of Afar, who participated in the Adwa battle with Emperor Minilik against the Italians. He also defeated the invading Egyptian army led by Ismail Basha to conquer Ethiopian lands. Sultan Alimirah himself, as a young man in Awsa, joined the group of young Ethiopians who resisted the Italian occupation of Ethiopia. After the defeat of Italy by the Ethiopians, Sultan Alimirah, together with his brother-in-law Yayo Hamadu, were amongst the Afar people who welcomed the victorious return of the Emperor Haile Sellossie in Addis Ababa.

At that time, Mohamed Yayo, the uncle of Sultan Alimirah, was the sultan of Awsa. The Afar elders, however, including Yayo Hamadu, suggested that the young Alimirah replace his uncle as Amoyta (sultan). Emperor Haile Sellossie accepted their recommendation and gave the title of *Dajazmach* to Sultan Alimirah and the title of *Fitawrare* to his brother-in-law Yayo Hamadu. He also gave them a well-trained brigade from his bodyguard army, headed by a general, in case Sultan Mohamed resisted to handing over power to his nephew.

After several days of journeying, they arrived in Aysaita in the dark of the night. They spent the night in Aysaita, while Sultan Alimirah stayed behind. Fitawrari Yayo Hamadu and his followers, together with the trained military officers who accompanied them, left for Hennale, where the palace of Sultan Mohamed was located. The next morning, however, they were faced with unexpected resistance. They found Sultan Mohamed sick in bed. The military officers who accompanied Sultan Alimirah took Sultan Mohamed to Addis Ababa while Hamadu stayed behind.

In 1945, Sultan Alimirah officially became the Amoyta (sultan) of the Afar people. What happened to Sultan Mohamed Yayo, however, is a story that will be discussed some other time.

After becoming the sultan, Alimirah was faced with several challenges. His aim was to create a peaceful and united environment for all Ethiopians everywhere and for the Afar people in particular. He worked to bring modern education and agricultural and economical development to the towns in Awsa. Toward the end of the 1960s, Awsa became a prosperous area in Ethiopia. A lot of Afars became cotton farmers and settled in Aysaita, Dubti, Baadu, and Daat Bahari. Many Ethiopians from other regions also became farmers and settled in several areas of the Afar region. The sultan established the Awsa Farmers Association and borrowed money from the Addis Ababa bank, whose general manager, Ato Debebe Yohanes, was his personal friend. Together they invested a lot of money in Awsa and the Baadu areas, also distributing money amongst farmers. At that time, Awsa was known as the "little Kuwait" because of its prosperity.

In 1974 when the Derg took power in Addis Ababa and invaded Awsa in June of that year, the sultan left behind over sixty tractors, eight bulldozers, and three Cessna planes. One of the three Cessna planes was piloted by the sultan's cousin, a trained Afar pilot by the name of Hanfare Ali Gaz.

Seventeen years later, when Derg was defeated and the sultan returned to Ethiopia, none of those things existed anymore. Several people had been killed and many things destroyed. The sultan tried to start from scratch, but things were very tough.

In 1972 Sultan Alimirah was invited to visit the United States of America by the USAID through the State Department visitors program. I was one of the three Afars who was fortunate to accompany his highness, the sultan. I, as his personal assistant, Ali Ibrahim Yusef, his personal advisor, Hashim Jamal Ashami, his interpreter, the sultan himself, and the state department escort all visited fifteen states during our stay.

One of the places we visited was Chicago, Illinois, where the sultan visited Operation Push, later called the Rainbow Coalition, which was led by Jesse Jackson, a well-known African-American activist at that time. When the sultan arrived there, he was given a standing ovation as he talked about the Ethiopian history and his admiration of the leadership of Emperor Haile Sellossie. The sultan was extremely impressed by this. The sultan also visited Elijah Mohamed, leader of the Black Muslims at that time, and met several state department officials. On our visit to Lubbock, Texas, we were given honorary American citizenship by the mayor of the city.

The American government and the American people we visited with the sultan were very welcoming and greeted us with great hospitality. The sultan expressed his extreme gratitude to the government of America and its people to the United States ambassador in Addis Ababa at that time. Very impressed with his visit, he called America the land of "milk and healthy young people."

As we went to the different states, the sultan was constantly asking if any Ethiopians lived there. In those days, not many Ethiopian lived in the States, but we met many students at the several universities we visited. Forty-five days later, the sultan left to visit London, while I stayed behind to continue my education at the American university in Washington, DC. After his visit to London, the sultan returned home.

In 1974, when the Derg came to power, Sultan Alimirah, being the reasonable man that he was, tried to reach some kind of understanding with the Derg leaders. He succeeded briefly in reaching an understanding with the Derg when General Amman Andom was the leader. Unexpectedly, however, the Derg killed General Amman Andom and more than sixty Ethiopian officials overnight. After that, it became clear to him that it was impossible for him to work with them. The sultan left Ethiopia through Djibouti to settle in Saudi Arabia, where King Khalid welcomed him and fifty of his followers.

During his stay in Saudi Arabia, he established the Afar Liberation Front (ALF), which fought the Derg regime for seventeen years alongside TPLF, OLF, ELF, EPLF, and several other ethnic groups fighting against the Derg dictatorship.

In 1991, after the fall of the Derg dictatorship, the sultan returned to Ethiopia and attended a July 1991 conference, together with his two sons, Hanfare and Ahmed Alimirah, as representatives of ALF and the rest of the Afar people. I attended the conference as an observer.

At the opening of the conference, the sultan discovered that the Eritrean leaders did not wish to participate in the conference as representatives but as observers. This he later understood was because of their wish to create a separate nation. This was news to the sultan, as he believed that after fighting Derg for so long, they all had the same intention of creating a peaceful, democratic, united country with equality for all. He was alarmed to see that this wasn't the case. To argue the point with the rest of the conference members, he raised his hand to be recognized and to state his opinion. When the chairman refused to recognize his presence and allow him to speak, the sultan grabbed a microphone from beside him and said:

"In my opinion, this conference was not to dismember Ethiopia but to unite Ethiopia¾a conference to discuss how to achieve equality, justice, democracy, and good governance for all Ethiopians. The Ethiopian people expect us to come out of this conference with a new government and democracy, not two different nations."

Isaias Aferworki, then leader of the Eritrean People's Liberation Front, stormed out of the room in anger.

The sultan then continued, saying, "If Eritreans are allowed a referendum for their future so that Ethiopians are allowed to decide, the voices of the Afar people should have particular significance, as a part of Afar land was part of the Eritrean province." He also claimed that he never wished to see Ethiopia landlocked.

The sultan lived every day for Ethiopian unity, and his loss was mourned by all of Ethiopia and neighboring countries.

I would like to take this opportunity as a dear family member and friend of the sultan to thank all of those who have expressed their condolences through various means. I would like to personally assure all Ethiopians that we, the family of the sultan and the Afar people, will follow in his footsteps and work for the peace and unity of the Ethiopian people!

The Era of Sultan Mohamed Yayo

As soon as sultan Mohamed Yayo took over power, he did not want to follow his father's dictatorial steps. he, therefore decided to share power with other people. He appointed Yayo Hammadu as his Deputy sultan or prime minister. He also appointed Mafak Hammadu to be in-charge of all Awsa farm land. Many other people were appointed as Malaks (or Ministers). At that time many of his father's political opponents were in Addis Ababa. Sultan Yayo had bad relationship with Queen Zawdito and Emperor Haile Sellassie. This explains why all the sultan's political opponents were taking to Addis Ababa.

Sultan Momahed wanted to change his father's policy. His intension was to forge good relationship with leaders in Shoa. So he went to Addis Ababa to meet to the Queen and her Crown Prince. In Addis Ababa he was accorded a befitting reception by the Queen and her Crown Prince. He told them about the death of his father, Sultan Yayo, and he told them that he wanted to create a good political relationship with them. They were pleased to see him take this kind of rare step. They thanked him for deciding not to follow his father's political policies for them. They conferred him the title of Dajazmach that was given to his father by the Emperor Mentlik II.

The Shoa leaders also pleaded with the political opponents of Sultan Yayo to forget the past grievances, go to Awsa and reconcile with Sultan Mohamed. As soon as Sultan Mohamed returned to Awsa. he gave the title Fitawrare to Yoyo Hammadu. Fitawrare means the Frontier' in Amharic. He also informed the people of Awsa that Yayo Hammadu had been appointed his accredited representative and could therefore speak on his behalf. He put it to them that anyone obedient to him was equally obedient to him, the Sultan, and vice versa. Yayo Hammadu was very strong and courageous man. The people of Awsa liked him and they did follow him.

Once when sultan Mohamed was visiting Addis Ababa there were some of his cousins who sued him to the Emperor Haile Sellassie for the things his father did to them.

His cousins who were suing him that time were very poor people. The needed some money. To get it they asked for another cousin, Allo Mohamed Aydahis, who was neutral in both sides to get them out of their financial mess. He then borrowed some money from an Arabian friend and promised him that he would repay it on a certain date. Unfortunately he could not redeem the promise. The creditor went to the court and the court ordered Allo to be detained until the money was repaid.

One of Sultan Mohamed Assistants came running to him. He said, "I have good news for you, sir"

The Sultan asked him, "What is the good news"

He replied, "I heard that Allo who was assisting and financing your cousins, our enemies, is in jail. He is in jail because he could not pay back the money he borrowed to finance your cousins against you".

But unexpectedly. Sultan Mohamed told his assistant he did consider that to be a good news. He said "We, of the Aydahisso tribe, do hurt each other but we do not allow others to hurt any of us. So, let us go and see where they are holding Allo." The guards told their leaders when they saw Sultan Mohamed at the prisons where Allo was being held. The leaders came running and they told the sultan, "please, Your excellence, you will have to go back home, we will bring him home to you "The sultan paid all money Allo owed to Arabian.

From that Allo and Sultan Mohamed reconciled. Allo swore to oath that he would never constitute any opposition to him again in his life. He later told his children to always remain neutral and never take sides in any dispute concerning cousins. His children are keeping up that neutrality up till today. Sultan Mohamed was good and very well cultured gentleman.

After a while Italy conquered Ethiopia. Emperor Haile Sellassie fled the country. Sultan Mohamed had to think for Awsa by himself. He chose accommodation with Italy. He told the Italian, "You are welcome to Awsa, to give protection from external aggression but please do not interfere in my internal affairs as the leader of my people"

While Mohamed was busy discussing with the Italian on how best to save his country from the occupation or complete domination of Italian, his half brothers, namely Kada Mohamed, Onda Mohamed and Aydahis Yayo, were planning to overthrow him. When Mohamed learnt of this he summoned them for a meeting. But they refused to honour his invitation for a meeting He wanted to order his soldiers to arrest all of them and bring them to him but for the fact they also had well armed soldiers for their own. As he was lingering over the choice of what to do about them he remembered what his father told him in his sick bed just before he died. He remembered that his father said "I killed my brothers an my nephews but I do not want you to do what I did. I do not want you to kill your brothers. Please, do not kill my sons".

Sultan Mohamed wanted to abide by the wish of deceased father but in a situation like this he had to do something about his brothers otherwise, they would not overthrow him to take power from him but they would also assassinate him. In fact, he had to act in self defence. So far protected hesitation he asked the Italian authorities to capture his rebellion brothers for him so as to prevent them from attacking him. The Italian soldiers were led by the sultan's loyalists, such as Fitawrare Yayo Hammadu. The Italian authorities asked his brothers and their followers to come out and surrender but they refused. Instead they attacked the Italian and Italian soldiers returned fire for fire. In the exchange of fire that ensued Kada Mohamed lost his life, Ahaydis Yayo got seriously wounded. Onda Mohamed and rest surrendered and they all were captured and taken prisoners of war(POWs) in Massawa. After they had spent a year in prison, Sultan Mohamed pardoned his brothers and returned them to Awsa. A few months later Onda Mohamed and Ahdahis Mohamed plotted to overthrow the sultan. Again sultan's soldiers captured them and they were imprisoned in Tigary. After some time again the sultan released them and were brought back to Awsa.

After a short while Onda Mohamed and Aydahia Mohamed revolted again. This time they left Awsa and went to Biro where had settled for some time. There they recruited ten people with whom they were to go to Awsa to assassinate Sultan Mohamed. On reaching a field, called Gayale, which was a huge desert field, one of the sultan's soldiers, Asa Gado, saw them. He altered some fellow Afar tribesmen loyal to the sultan. They rallied round and attacked them. Aydahis Yayo was again wounded and this time captured. Onda Mohamed and his followers, some to them badly wounded, surrendered and were taken to captives to the sultan. The Sultan this time decided to imprisoned them in Awsa, specifically in the place called Hammadi Puri. Sultan Mohamed asked them "How on earth do you think that only with ten untrained people from Biru you can overthrow the sultan of Awsa, the most powerful Afar leader with all his brilliant and determined soldiers"?.

Onda Mohamed said, "We thought nobody would suspect us. We are sorry. We made a mistake." This time sultan did not release them from jail. They remained until sultan was overthrown by sultan Alimirah and Fitawrare Yayo Hammadu.

During the short-lived Italian occupation Ethiopia, Sultan Mohamed was invited to Rome to see Mussolini at tea time. When he went there he took a large entourage with him. Among them Fitawrare Yayo Hammadu, at that time who was considered the number 2 in Awsa at the time, Alwan Yayo, his nephews, Kurba Hamamdu and other thirty dignitaries.

Italy had cordial relationship with Awsa people. The Italians allowed the people of Awsa to administer to themselves. When Italy was defeated after the Second World War and Emperor Haile Sellassie returned to Ethiopia, the Ethiopian officials were capturing the defeated Italian Soldiers all over the country and taking them to the Emperor as a present.

Some Afar officials told the Sultan he should do the same. But the Sultan objected saying, "We had warm relationship with Italy. If these soldiers like to stay here with us they are welcome. If they want to go somewhere else, they should go in peace. Nobody should bother them. The only thing I can do for the Emperor Haile Sellossie is to go and welcome him myself but not to take and Italian or Italians to him as other officials are doing."

Some Afar officials, including Fitawrare Yayo Hammadu, who was Number 2 Citizen in Afar at the time, were opposed to the decision taken by the Sultan. Later on the Fitawrare took his followers with him and went to surrender the Italian leader in Awsa at that time, Colonel Rowdy. But the Colonel told them, "The Sultan told me that I do not have to surrender. He gave me his word that I would be protected by him." Fitawrare Yayo insisted that he should surrender or else they would be forced to surrender. The Italians resisted but were overpowered. Fitawrare Yayo took 999 Italian soldiers hostage and presented them to the Emperor as a welcome gift to him.

This action marked the beginning of the misunderstanding brewing between Sultan Mohamed and Fiawrare Yayo. The Sultan himself did not go to Addis Ababa to welcome the Emperor back from the exile and to congratulate him but his officials were went in turns to see the Emperor.

Emperor Haile Sellossie used to send messages to the Sultan telling him to come to Addis Ababa to see him promising him befitting reception. But the Sultan kept on replying that he was sick and that as suck he would not be able to honour his invitation. As a matter of fact, the two leaders could not meet. Fitawrare Yayo was a personal friend to Emperor Haile Sellossie. For him it was an excellent thing that the Italians were defeated and the Emperor went back to Ethiopia.

With the deterioration of the relationship between Sultan Mohamed and Fitawrare Yayo Hammadu he decided to remove him from his position as Number 2 Citizen and appoint another fellow, Assyaytu. When Yayo heard that, he became furious and told the Sultan, "Lubak-Elle-Akke-Kalol-Wakri-Wakri-Makkah." (Meaning, I have been known in this land of ours as a lion. I do not want to be known as a rat.)

From that day Fitawrare Yayo Hammadu began to work towards overthrowing the Sultan while the Sultan was, on his own part, very eager to get rid of him by the easiest means available.

Incidentally, Fitawrare Yayo Hammadu was married to Fatuma Hanfare who happened to be a niece of Sultan himself. She has a younger brother whose name was Alimirah, presently sultan Alimirah. Fitawrare Yayo Hammadu consulted his friend, Haile Sellassie, secretly and intimated was him with ongoing-on between his brother (the sultan) and himself. The emperor himself was unhappy with sultan. He was looking for a way to remove him from his position. So when he heard of the misunderstanding between the sultan and Yayo tyhre felt that long-awaited opportunity has knoked. This, of course, was evident in his advice to Yayo, thus: "Since you are his number2,you cannot overthrow him and become the sultan yourself. I can assure of my unflinching support for the accomplishment of this arduous task"

Fitawrare expressed to him the fear that people of Awsa will not accept him as their sultan. This, he said, was because traditional sultan must come from Aydahisso tribe and that since he was not from that tribe he was not going to face serious resistance from the people to get to his nefarious end. He, however said he had an idea of a way out of it. Said, he "I have a brother-in-law from Aydahisso tribe. In fact, he is a nephew of sultan himself. He young man of 22 years. I can be his guardian until he matures, but it be better if he becomes the sultan. People will accept and welcome him. There will be no opposition. There will be no animosity."

He succeeded in convincing the emperor and he agreed with him and he went back to Awsa it inform his brother-in-law, Alimirah, of the discussion he had with the emperor. Alimirsh agreed with him and was poised to ascend the sultanate throne.

Meanwhile, Sultan Mohamad never wind of plans being put to gather against him. He sent a message to Fitawrare Yayo Hammadu asking him to accompany him on a tour to Hammadi Buri on the following Thursday. It was speculated that Sultan Mohamed intended to eliminate Fitawrare as soon as they got to Hamadi Buri. Fitawrsre was not a fool. He knew what the sultan was doing. On the appointed Thursday instead of following sultan to Hammadi Buri, we went straight to Emperor Haile Sellassie in Addis Ababa taking along with him the young ASlimirah and a handful of other trusted lieutenants.

When sultan heard of what had happened he ordered his soldiers after them and bring them back either dead or alive. Unknowingly they were dealing with very witty Fitawrare who had already planned and escaped very neatly. He arranged with the Emperor to meet them at Hadodas, in Mile.

By the time sultan's soldiers arrived there they had left in a car. All the sultan said was "Let them go." By the time they are tired of the cold weather and the insect bite they will be forced to come back to Awsa.

Either because sultan was sick or because he did not have educated people around him or may still for other reason, it seemed, he did not appreciate the extent of the seriousness of the situation. Consequently, it was after hesitating for several days that he decided to send a delegation to Addis Ababa to see the Emperor and other important officials. The delegation was headed by Data Assiaytu and Mohamed Abadar.

Assisytu was unenlightened and did know anything. Although Mohamed Abadar was literate, his loyalty to sultan was very questionable: he could better judged more loyal to Fitwarare Yayo Hammadu.

The sultan to the delegation to Addis Ababa that he had done nothing to the Emperor Hail Sellassie nor to his officials and he was therefore surprised as to why the Amhara officials kept on creating administrative problem for him when he always given them(Amhara Officials) butter and honey whenever they were in need of them. He then instructed the delegation to take along with them a lot of butter, honey and money saying "when you get there, devide the items among them. Bribe all of them and tell them to send Fitawrare Yayo Hammadu and his men back to Awsa.

The Sultan's delegation went to Addis Ababa as planned and bribed every Amhara official, except the Emperor himself, with the items which he instructed them to take along with them. They divided the honey among the Amhara s in the name of Sultan Mohamed but the money in the name Fitawrare Yayo Hammadu. Eventually the credit went to Mohamed Abaderta and Fitawrare for bringing and sharing money to them.

Abaderta betrayed Sultan Mohamed, instead of talking on behalf of the sultan that trusted him and sent him on a such delegation he allied with his opponents and gave them wrong information about Sultan Mohamed. Sultan Mohamed asked Abaderta to tell the Emperor Haile Sellassie he did not come to see him in Addis Ababa because he was seriously sick and that as soon as he recovered (which was unlikely because of the gravity of the illness)he would immediately come and see him.

It was very clear to Mohamed Abaderta that the sultan was speaking the truth but because of his friendship with Fitawrare Yayo he preferred to present the reverse side of sultan's statement. He said that sultan was simply feigning illness. He also accused him of wanting to sell Awsa to France. as Assyatu and others who were him could not could not communicate in Amharic nor in any other language, they were compelled to believe whatever Abaderta told them. This was the major detrimental role which ignorance played in the delegation.

Mohamed Abaderta reported to them that he distributed all the money, gold and butter to all the important Amhara official in accordance with the sultan's directives. He also said that he actually reported them that the sultan could not come to Addis Ababa because he was ill. He concluded by telling them that Amhara official were very satisfied with the sultan and that they had no ill feeling against him.

Assayaytu had no cause whatsoever to disbelieve Mohamed Abaderta reports, Thereafter, they went back to gather to Awsa. There, they gave the sultan the same report. The sultan was glad that he could strike a compromise with the Emperor and his officials. He had no knowledge of delegation's betrayal of his confidence. This betrayal could be more dangerous than any other harm that could be intended by any political opponent against him.

Later Emperor Haile Sellassie summoned a meeting of his official Fitawrare Yayo Hammadu the agenda of which was how they could oust Sultan Mohamed. At the meeting Fitawrare Yayo Hammadu informed them that the sultan isolated from all his officials. Said he, "He was alone with his wife, Madina Isse. There is not going be any resistance in Awsa because nobody is with the Sultan. What I need is a small number of soldiers and the Emperor's blessings. "

Fitawrare Yayo Hammadu knew what he was talking about. Since the Sultan removed him as his Number 2 man in the Sultanate consequent upon series of political logjams, he had not appointed a effective replacement for his position. Assyaytu was not a match for Fitawrare Yayo and this explained why he was very confidently telling the emperor that there would not be aby resistance.

Although, as earlier stated, Fitawrare Yayo Hammadu was not an educated man, he was naturally very intellegent. He was known in Awsa not only for his astuteness but also for his courage and fearlessness. His leadership was well accepted by all of the people in Awsa. When the sultan suddenly dismissed him from his position and appointed Assyaytu a lot of people were highly surprised and despondent.

Six months later, after serious consultation and planning, Emperor Haile Sellassie decided to give his backing to Fitawrare yayo Hammadu and Alimirah Hanfare (later Sultan Alimirah I) to overthrow Sultan Mohamed. The emperor Conferred on Alimirah the title Dajazmach and he restored the title of Fitawrare to Fitawrare Yayo Hammadu. He did not stop with these mind-boosting conferment of titles, he gave them thousands of well trained Kuburzabagna (body guards and soldiers) to enable them to go to Awsa and effectively remove Sultan Mohamed from power, and crush any resistance that might stand on their way to achieving this objective. It took them about a fortnight to reach Aysaita. One of the tactics they used as narrated by the people who took in the operation was that they took several empty trucks along with them and whenever they saw an afar man or woman they would capture him or her and put in a truck and take them away in the trucks. This they continued until they arrived at Aysaita. By doing this they were able to control the infiltration to anybody in Awsa of the news that they coming to invade Sultan Mohamed before their arrival. All of these events took place in the year 1947.

They also prevented any trucks, cars, camels, etc, and anybody from going beyond Bati. Sultan Mohamed did quite unaware of this development. He himself was living in Hinnale Place while his older children were staying in the Gargory Palace.

One Saturday in the evening when the Fitawrare-led army started crossing the huge desert field of Gayale situated between Sando and Aysatia towns, Kadda Yayo saw the lights of the invaders' trucks. He noticed that the number of cars were unusually many. He also observed that they were military trucks. With all these observation he understood that it was an invasion army. He woke up his brothers who were then asleep and together they went to the Hinnale Palace to see their father and tell them what they saw.

On getting Kadda Yayo told his father all what he saw. He also told him with ever assurance that they trucks he saw were military trucks. Kadda Yayo did not mince words in telling his father that the people he saw were detailed to come and overthrow him and take over the government of Sultanate.

"Who wants to overthrow me? What for? Emperor Haile Sellassie would not do that. You just have to go back and sleep."

Kadda Yayo went back but could not go back to slee. After a short while he went back to his father with the same colpaint saying, "father, you must believe me. They are coming to fight us. Fitawrare Yayo hammadu is with them.

But the Sultan said, "No, who is Firawrare Yayo Hammadu? Because of him, I don't believe that Emperor Haile Sellassie and the Amhara Officials in Addis Ababa.

Kadda Yayo said, "Father let us at least order your soldiers and bodyguards to come and resist them."

"No", the Sultan insisted.

At this point in time, Kadda Yayo could no longer take chances. He, therefore, ordered Sultan's bodyguards and soldiers to come out and protect the Sultan.

When the Sultan heard what Kadda Yayo did, he was furious. He dismissed all the soldiers and bodyguards who were around him and told Yayo, "If you are so scared that you can not go back to sleep you can come and sleep under my bed here."

TO Kadda Yayo, this statement was grievous slight on his personality. He replied his father, "Alright, you will see what I am talking about tomorrow."

The invaders arrived the Sultan's Palace at Hinnale, without any resistance, Early in the morning the following day. When they entered the Palace it was a lone guard that attempted resistance when some shots.

Like to advise you on one thing. It is true that our fathers have killed each other. We have inherited bad reputation in our Aydahisso family. Everybody says that the propel of Aydahisso hate each other. I want to tell you and ask you not to kill my children.

Sultan Alimirsah accepted and gave him assurance that he will not kill his children. They both had coffee together and after that the officers themselves took the deposed Sultan Mohamed with them to Addis Ababa while the new sultan stayed behind in Aysaita to rule the country.

Fitawrare Yayo Hammadu also stayed behind in Awsa as the new Sultan's assistant, Since Alimirah was only a young man of 22 years old, Fitsawrare Yayo who was much older was the de facto leader of the country.

The Childern Of Sultan Mohamad

Sultan Mohamed fathered about 37 male and female children from several wives. But here only those of them, five in numbers, who followed their father to Addis Ababa, will featured. They include, Kadda Yayo Mohamed, Kadda Alimirah Mohamed, Kadda Allo Mohamed, Kadda Aydahis Mohamed and Hanfare Mohamed.

Kadda Yao was the oldest of these five children. He was groomed by his father to succeed him after death. That time nobody thought of the forceful change of leadership in Awsa.

Led by Kadda Yayo, the children of Sultan Mohamed went to Handag area where a lot Afar propel went to settle.

Many people wanted to resist the takeover but since all the afar leadership conspired with Fitarare Yayo, Sultan Mohamed's children and all those behind them were fast to see that there was not much they could do against the majority.

Initially they did not know what to do, finally Kadda Yayo decided to follow his father and relate to Emperor Haile Sellassie their own side of long story. He wanted to flee friends and foes alike but this way was not easy for them. To be able to do that he consulted a local magician named Ado Hummad. This magician made the place so dark that with the exception of those people who were trying to escape, nobody else could see even his palm. But those escaping with the deposed Sultan Mohamed were able to see very clearly. In the face of this artificial impenetrable darkness Kadda Yayo, his brothers and their trusted followers escaped their people and lived in Addis Ababa.

It is this writer's opinion that that Kadar Yayo took a wrong decision by following his father, he should have resisted right there and then. When they reached Batti an officer there arrested them and took them to the Emperor on the trumped up charge that he caught them organizing resistance against Emperor. As a reward to the officer for a job well done, The Emperor decorated him while he sent Kadda Yayo, his brothers and his followers to the prisons.

For about one year they did not see their father. Finally when they met their father, the deposed Sultan Mohamed realised that he not only made mistake but that he also toyed with his throne by refusing to listen to his, Kadda Yayo when he came to him several times informing him of the impeding danger of invasion organized by Emperor Haile Sellassie. By so doing he misused the ample opportunity given him to crush the invasion.

After his deposition, the ex Sultan Mohamed was taken to the hospital where he was adequately treated. When he had recovered he had the opportunity to meet with the Emperor. As the deposed Sultan not could speak Amharic they had to hire somebody else who was also taking treatment in Addis Ababa to serve as an interpreter.

This man, whose name was Hadji Gazali, was a prominent man in Awsa. He could speak not only Afar but also Arabic fluently. While the deposed sultan spoke in Afar Hadji Gazali translated into Arabic and the third person who spoke in Arabic and Amharic translated into Amharic to the Emperor. Their conversation went thus:

Emperor: Mohamed you betrayed me

Mohamed: No, your Majesty, I did not, It was you who always betrayed your people. If I had betrayed you, would you think that you would catch me in(Afar-Ary) a house with my wife? I am not the first one you have betrayed many traditional leaders like me and you eliminated most of them physically.

Emperor: Do you deny that you have been invited to Rome and that in Rome. you met with an Italian leader, Mussolini?

Mohamed: I don't deny that, when Italy invaded Ethiopia your majesty fled to Europe with your family. As for me I had to take refuge in Italy to save my people from harm.

Emperor: Even now you are making frantic arrangement with France so you can bring French forces in Awsa.

Mohamed: That is an unfounded speculation. You remember that I was the one who fiercely fought France in Oduma and I too stopped from Afambo. I personally do not want to have to do with France. It will therefore be outrageous for anyone to accuse me for trying to bring France in Awsa.

Emperor: Whatever happened has happened. For now I will send you to your country, Awsa.

Mohamed: That is alright.

Therefore he went back to where was staying.

According to Balambaras Assa Hummad, one evening the Sultan was visited by three men one of whom was medical doctor. The doctor wanted to administer injection to the Sultan but, being very suspicious of the true intention of the men and coupled with fact that Sultan was feeling fine that day, I vehemently objected. I told them that Sultan did not require any medication. But they were unyielding. When Sultan said "If the doctor prescribes injection for me let administer it" the doctor went ahead to implement his nefarious plans. At this point in time they asked me to give them some privacy to treat Sultan.

Balambaras Assa-Hummad said, "I went outside in compliance with the doctor's instructions believing that those men will kill the sultan ever before he came back. But to my utter surprise I came back to meet him alive, even feeling fine. I thanked God that he was alright. The three men departed after administering the injection to him.

"I then served him with dinner and then coffee after which I went over to my room leaving him to sleep"

"The following day in the morning when I came back to wake him up as usual, I saw him lying stone dead on his bed. When I saw this I did not need anybody to tell me what has chanced I was cock sure that the doctor and his men poisoned the Sultan".

Sultan Mohamed was buried in Gollalle area of Addis Ababa. This brings to a conclusion of storey about Sultan Mohamed.

The Childern Of Sultan Mohamed

Sultan Mohamed married several women and, as should be expected, begot about 37 offspring most of whom were menthe eldest ones among them include, Kadda Yayo, Kadda Almirah, Kadda Allo, Kadda Aydahis and Hanfare.

These five children together with their followers accompanied their father to Addis Ababa where they were imprisoned with hardened criminals for a year. They were released but were not allowed to move outside Addis Ababsa. Their cases were lefty to the Crown prince, Asfaw-Wassen, as he was the overall leader of Wallo of Wallo Provinces and Awsa was part of Wallo instead of solving their problems The Cron Prince and his men used them ageist Sultan Alimirah and Fitawra re Yayo Hammadu.

Whenever they needed money, butter or anything else from Awsa they called on Fitawrare Yayo Hammadu and ask him to bring them those things or els. "we will have no choice other than to send these innocent children of former sultan back to their country."

Fitawrare Yayo would say "No please", I will give whatever you want from Awsa". Based on that he would give several barrels of butter and lot of money. When that was done they leave them until the supplies are exhausted. As soon as they exhausted the supplies they would repeat the demand in their usual way of doing sodas usual they would not fail to receive. They kept on extorting different items from the children of the former sultan in this way again and again.

Meanwhile one of their brothers, Hanfare, fall sick and died in Addis Ababa. Later Allo died too. For about 35 years they lived n suffered under the house arrest in Addis Ababa until Emperor Haile Sellassie was overthrown by the dreg in 1974. As their followers they too suffered for a while but were finally sent back to Awsa in military trucks.

Maad Aradaytu (Maad Bara), one of the followers of Sultan Mohamed's children, made a consultation with a fortune teller (Kalluwalle) whose name was Biru. In fact when the Sultan was captured and taken to Hinnale by invaders Maad Bary was not around. He said he was out on a date. He said that he was very angry when he learnt that the Sultan had left the country with all his children. Then he said that he became somehow happy when later he was informed that the Sultan left but did not go with his children. This was the time when he decided to join Kadda Yayo and other brothers. He said he stopped on the Mountain of Gargory, saying, "We bid farewell to our beautiful Kallo, the fertile land. Since our leader Kadda Yayo chose to be diplomatic we went to Shoa. In Addis Ababa we met some blacks who were so huge that they look as if they would swallow someone. There we also met the whites who would kill without mercy. But nobody dared to look into the eyes Kadda Yayo not come nor come very close to us. Right from the beginning we were caught unawares because we trusted Kurba who was at Tandho."

"We thought that Kurba was with us but we were betrayed by him. Then because we sent Assyaytu to Shoa to negotiate on the Sultan's behalf with the Shoa leaders and because we we reported to us that the Shoa leaders wrote a favourable letter to the Sultan we became unsuspicious and were subsequently caught unawares. What was impossible for the entire Kallo could not be possible for me. But one thing I can take credit for and boast of is the fact that I stood by my Sultan till he bred his last. In fact, he died on my laps. I thought that I did what I was supposed to do. But one thing is that when one was young one imagines so much and thinks he might accomplish so much, now I understand that us only a wish and a wish only remains as a wish." This is what he said in Afar thus:

"Agby Hagidit Sugneh
Misly Forey Eyeneh
Orry Forey Eyeneh
Wakrih Ennah Howerisak Nemeteh
Younguly Ennah Kookoousak Nemeteh
Wowaedi Nabam Ninebem Tobe
Misly Foreh Eyeneh
Orry Raeh Eyeneh
Wowaedi Nabam Nikhinem Tobe
Gargorik Amol Solleh
Kalloh Salam Abneh
Salamat Abneh
Sirat Abnaeye Kadda Yayoy
Alefan Nufkunem Tobe
Bateyan Daar Namete Waedi
Datmary Sinam Yakme Neh Sugaymy
Yayok Enty Waktonu Yefferenih
Nek Bagul Sinam Tawo Teffereh
Ambary Koraesy Yayok Enneh
Addis Ababa Akakeyan Daar Nemete Waedi
Datmary Sinam Yakme Neh Sugayh
Admary Sinam Edda Nehsugayh
Tonnah Yayok Enty Waktonu Yefferneh
Nek Bagul Sinam Tawoterrereh
Kurby Tandahot Yani Naylahisseh
Asyayti Alet Yanni Naylahisseh
Misly Yok Gurumbal Rabeh
Askartu Migae Dudem Akalemy
Kalo Tefferem Effere Kal
Furrayni Neyay Odirik Tanih Tan
Yaniay Odirik Tanih Tan."

The lady fortune tell (Biru or Kalluwalle) assured him back. She said:

"Sin Hinnay Sin Abobti Yeynebeh Yen
Yatlaw Kalo Gory Malymbarinneh
Shoa Galto Malym Barynneh
Yab Mohamadak Yabali Mayaysay
Yab Mohamadak Yabali Mayaysay
Aly Dayloy Dabab Naboby Kenik Itte."

(Meaning: We understood that the Shoa leaders had no condition while the people of Kallo had no appreciation. Sultan Mohamed took care of not you alone but your parents as well. Uncle Alli is not better than Uncle Mohamed. You people, you are animals and the children of animals.)

In Afar a lady fortune teller is called "Kalluwalle" while her male counterpart is called "Ginnily". At that time there were two reputable "Ginnelies" in Awsa. Before Sultan Mohamed was overthrown he went to Shoa for consultation with the Queen of Ethiopia and Taz Tafari. Because he did not come back soon his people wanted to know why he was not back. So they consulted these two "Ginnilies", one of whom was Dolab while the other was Muray.

Usually the fortune teller would meditate. While in meditation, some people asked Muray to tell them what was responsible for the Sultan's protracted delay in coming home to his country.

Muray, on his own part, told them that the Sultan was busy paving t way of reconciling with the Shoa leaders and that he would be back home as soon as he completed the arrangements. He concluded by telling them that the Sultan would be back very soon.

His counterpart, Dolab, was of an entirely different view. Said he, "The Sultan has become lame, he can now sit but cannot stand and not walk. In conclusion, the Sultan will come back but he is not going to come back any soon; certainly not in the Ramadan month or in the month that follows Ramadan. He is not coming back in summer not winter; he is not coming back in spring nor autumn but he will be back later."

Later the Sultan came back and when all that fortune tellers said were narrated to him he sent for the two of them. He decorated Muray for saying that the Sultan will be back soon, but to Dolab he said, "You saw in your vision and told the people i would be back soon. You were right about that but didn't you see that I am going to shave your beard and your forehead too?"

He shaved his beard and his forehead as he said. Below are the statements of the fortune tellers in Afar language:

Muray: "Gahele Gititte Yaymaekalah
                     Gahelenugussosahorakalah"

Dolab: "Yangude Aran Meme Hinneh
                     Daffey Noum Solle Hinneh
                     Somut Mayan
                     Some Futrit Mayan
                     Hagayat Mayan
                     Hagay Bahet Mayan
                     Gilalat Mayan
                     Gilal Bahe Mayan."

Once Mr. Dolab, the fortune teller, was meditating in the middle of the big crowd. Suddenly he saw his wife having an affair with another man. He asked someone among the crowd, "Do you see, another man is having an affair with my wife?" the man asked him, "How do I see that when I am here with you?" Said Mr. Dolab, just step aside because I see it myself."

He went to his house where he found another man with his wife. The exchange of words ensued between them in Afar:

Dolab: Rakub Addo Yokradam Table

The man: Marot Kunnahanih Mahakablem

Dolab: Lenum Yableh Yanih Afakahhab

On some other occasion when Dolab was in meditation he saw in his vision that someone had just killed his nephew. When he woke up from his meditation, ran to the place where he saw his nephew killed and revenged the death of his nephew by murdering the murderer. Then he was arrested and put in the Hammadi Bury prisons by Sultan Mohamed. He remained there until Sultan Mohamed was toppled before he was not only released but also pardoned by Sultan Alimirah through the general amnesty he granted to all prisoners.

Dolab also had the following words with another man in Afar:

The man: Olueto Dolabow Yesabohgary

Dolab: Kiedoh Obokemtabaryok Teregy

The man: Amo Asalek Wadrih Maskatteyo

Dolab: Abu Ma Kodda Rukam Yokta Kaleh

The man: Dean Aloytak Kaleh Baral Leeyoh

Dolab: Maha Wayta Hay Arah Gaytehtanih

The man: Walal Labhak Kaleh Leeyoh

Dolab: Maha Waytu Hay Walal Gaytehtanih

The man: Gile Kiely Godam Yoktekeh

Dolab: Kukataysaway Gabat Mabrad Maly

The man: Bagytome kala Yokyekeh

Dolab: Habelek Edah Hanat Hulbat Hayes

Dolab predicted that there were going to be a lot of wars, leading to a horrifying blood bath and a period of anguish for the Afar people but whoever survived at the end would enjoy a good life.

This is what Dolab told them in Afar:

"Asanat Sharia Siasak Merelon

Asagaladay Gabanok Gurelon

Tout Garbisillah Adak Merelow."

While he was still alive the Issas, the Somali speaking tribe that were living in their neighbourhood invaded some part of Afar Region, and did that all the time, and took "Akkaly", the She Camels that were associated with the Awsa supernatural powers.

The Awsa people were furious and by the leadership of Fitawrare Yayo Hammadu, the second man in command to Sultan Alimirah and Mohamed Mirah (Kadda Mohamadihbara) they launched a counter attack and invaded the areas inhabited by prisoners of war while several others were seriously injured. They not only returned their "Akkaly" Camels but also brought a lot of camels, cows and goats that belonged to the Issas. Dolab showered the following praises in Afar language on the leaders of the invasion:

"Ankarara Mirahow Nimirahow

Mirahow Ayromalow

Bakar Malow

Olul Meow

Neforsay,"

Dolab also predicted his own demise. He said very soon he would be put in a house that would be built for him by some men. This, he said, was not because he liked to change the house in which he was then living but because he had no power to object to any proposal for him to move into the new house. Said he, "That will be house in which i will dwell forever"

He went further, "I predict that good things will be coming for the Afar people and I myself will partake of them." The following is what he said in Afar language:

"Ann Temete Maanek Nahar Ekke

Kalok Raetem Bara

Harir Ennale."

No one would at this point like to know what happened to Sultan Mohamed's children who followed him to Addis Ababa

As stated earlier, at the initial state they were considered criminals by the authorities in Addis Ababa. The fact that they were children of the Sultan was just sufficient to incriminate them. They were, however, later released and pardoned by Emperor Haile Sellassie who restricted their movement to within Addis Ababa where they remained under house arrest till the Derg took power from the Emperor on September 1, 1974. That was 35 years later.

While they were incarcerated in Addis Ababa two of their brothers, Hanfare and Allo died of natural causes. However, Kadda Yayo, Kadda Alimirah and Aydahis survived the Emperor.

In the beginning Colonel Mangistu and his Derg officers summoned them to their office and sent them to Awsa to calm things down there. Colenel Mangistu reminded to then the agonies they went through during the regime of Emperor Hail Sellassie and Sultan Alimirah. He told them that the time had come up for them to work hard to calm down the Afar people in Awsa and explained to the people who was their best to calm down the people.

Kadda Yayo got married and settled in Berga area with his maternal relatives. Things became much better for them until Colenel Mangistu found a group of Afar youngsters willing to work with him. Those youngsteres were made up of Jamal Addin, Abdul Kader Redo, Yusuf Yassin Mohamoda, Mohamoda Gaas, Ismael Said Ahmed, Musa Mohamed Abubakar among others. They were not only more academically educated but also more politically aware than Kadda Yayo and Kadda Alimirah

Colonel Mangistu, one of the most heartless leaders in Ethiopian history, forgot what Kadda Yayo and his brothers did for him hence he put Kadda Yayao in prison in Dessie. He did not stop there, he ordered Kadda Alimirah to leave Awsa. Kadda Alimirah left Awsa, as ordered by Mangistu, and sought asylum in Kombolcha. Jamal Abdul Kader Redo from Tio region in Eritrea was appointed in charge of all Afar affairs while Habib Mohamed, who was hither to working in Kombolcha area, was removed from Awsa.

Later, Colonel Mangistu wanted to create autonomous regions as he called them during his time. This was aimed at creating a buffer against the Eritreans. He did not want to hear the name Afar mentioned, therefore he called the area Assab region. Its capital, he said, should be Assab not Aysaita, because Sultan Alimirah and his resistance movement, Afar Liberation Front (A.L.F.), happened to be from Aysaita.

Those Afar youngsters that joined the Mangistu government did not want to be branded partial or unpatriotic against their own people of Afar. Thus they tried from time to time to see one thing or the other they could do to assuage the misery inflicted on them by Mangistu. This they found impossible because Mangistu was illiterate as well as ignorant sadist who would not want to listen to anything that could better the Afar people's lot.

Although he did not arrest any popular politician among his supporters, he did not make them feel

31

secured till he finally ran away, it was impossible for anybody to guess what Mangistu ans his men were up to.

However, the Afar youngsters that worked with Mangistu survived him. At the time of this writing Habib Mohamed and Jamal Abdul Kader Redo are still in detention in Addis Ababa. Mohameda Gaas had joined the opposition of the T.G.E and he is believed to somewhere either in Europe or Dhibouti. Yusuf Yassin is working with T.G.E He is stationed at the Ethiopian Embassy in Cairo as the Counsellor, while Kadda Yayo died in 1990 before the collapse of Derg. Kadda Alimirah died in 1992 at Gawany after the Derg regime had been ousted.

These two gentlemen suffered during the reign of Emperor Haile Sellassie and during the Derg government. In fact, they spent a better part of their life time suffering. Such was life and that is the end of their lives. Their brother, Kadda Aydahis, is living in Baadu area at this time and the rest of the Sultan Mohamed's children and grand children are still living in Awsa.

Yayo Hamadu

Yayo Hamadu was one of the greatest Afar people in Awsa.

He was born in Emminee and raised there, but his great-aunt Kadda Rokiya brought him to the Awsa area. He grew up there with her children. When her children were in power, he was a close assistant to the sultan Hanfare. When Sultan Hanfare and others of Rokiya's children were defeated by their brother, Sultan Yayo, Yayo Hamadu ran away to the Baadi area with Sultan Hanfare. When Sultan Hanfare was associated by the order of Sultan Yayo, Yayo Hamadu was there with him.

Later on, Yayo Hamadu returned to Awsa. He told this writer that he used to sleep outside of the sultan's palace. Sometimes sultan Yayo came out, and whenever he did, he saw Yayo Hamadu. Later on, when the sultan came out without his guards, he told Faradu, his palace chief, to let Yayo Hamadu sleep inside the palace. After that, he got *gibriyta*, the bread they distributed to the guards.

Eventually Yayo Hamadu started eating with Faradu himself. He became part of the sultan's inner circle of people, and the sultan sent him for all kinds of work. Yayo Hamadu was given the job of protecting the fertile grass for Sultan Yayo's cattle. By the time Sultan Yayo died, Yayo Hamadu was doing that job, and because he did it well, Sultan Mohamed, when he came to power, appointed him as his overall assistant.

Sultan Mohamed gave Yayo Hamadu his first cousin Okuby Kadafo to be his wife. That marriage could not last, so they divorced. Later, he married the niece of Sultan Mohamed: Fatuma Hanfare. That marriage lasted until he passed away. He was so proud of his wife, Fatuma, that he used to call her his "secret weapon." He used to say that he had two important things in his life¾his carbine gun and his wife, Fatuma. No one has yet been born who hasn't heard of Yayo Hamadu's claim about his carbine gun and his wife. He also said that anyone who was not lucky enough to marry a wife like Fatuma from Aydahsso, as he had, shouldn't claim to be married. Fitaurare Yayo Hamadu was a self-made, powerful person. He was a hero to many people in Awsa. He made us proud in many ways, even with all his shortcomings.

Later Yayo Hamadu got married Fatum Hanfare, the elder sister of Sultan Alimirah Who is currently the Sultan of Afar people. Fitawrare Yayo Hamadu served under sultan Alimirah. Through his god leadership he made name for himself and for the people and earned a lot of respect for himself. His interest in Afar and his defence of Afar territorial integrity against the Issas boosted his popularity. As far as he was concerned the Afar people ha d no enemy in the world except the Issas. That view was not shared by all afars. In his days if the Issa people took anything from an afar man Fitawrare would to his aid. He used to claim that whoever said that he had not heard of the grandson of Hamadi Allo, which is himself Yayo Hamadu, was yet to be born.

He also said once when he was going with a group of Afar people they were attacked by some enemies. He said there was a hill the place where the enemies attacked them and that some of the people to take cover in the hill while other took cover himself. According to him, while those who took cover by the hill were killed by the enemies those who were defended by him survived the attack.

He used to boast that he got the best wife a man could get." if a surprised guest arrives at our home "he said," my wife will take care of that". I have a trusted wife, Fatum Hanfare, and a trusted gun, Carbine".

Fitawrare Yoyo died in 1973 at the ripe age of 84 years of age. His friends, Emperor Haile Sellassie, Sult Alimirah and other dignitaries of the Ethiopian government at that time attended his funeral ceremony. This self-made proud son of Afar made every Afar proud of him by the services he rendered to his people. That too, endeared him to all Afar people.

Fitawrare Yayo was survived by the male children, Ahmed Yayo, Hassan Yayo and Ali Yayo, from different wives. Unfortunately his trusted and favourite wife, Fatum Hanfare, had no for him. The third Ali Yayo was killed by the derg while the other two are still live and are both living in Awsa.

Alwan Mohamed, Alwan Yayo, Alwan Aydahis, Alwan SAlimirah and Alwan Abdulkader, were offspring of Alwan and his wife, Fatum. They were and are all still famous in Awsa. Mohamed and Yayo were the most popular. Their mother is a daughter of Sultan Alimirah I The man who ousted Mohamed Aydahis from power and became Sultan of Awsa with the help of Yemen. Their father, Alwan, was from the tribe called Adali Sheikha in Assab Area. It was suspected that he was one of those who helped Alimirah I to get assistance from the Yemen at that time. Afterthe death of AlimiramI Alwan became the friend of Sultan Yayo who wedded the Alimirah's daughter, Fatuma. She bore him three sons-Alwan Mohamed, Alwan Yayo and Alwan Aydahis.

Alwan Mohamed and Alwan Yayo were very close to close to Sultan Mohamed. They accompanied him to vey trip he took both within and outside of the county. Even when he travelled to Rometo meet Mussolini they both were in entourage.

After the fall of Mohamed The Alwan boys joined Sultan Alimirah II and his deputy Fitawrare Yayo Hamadu. They were among the Sultan trusted officials.

Alwan Mohamed the Deputy leader of Afar men in Awsa. Wheever there was war between Awsa Afars and the neighboring tribes it was Alwan Mohamed who gave orders to Awakala to prepare themselves to defend Awsa. His position was known as Fie Madagayna(Deputy leader of the Association). While the leader of Awakala or the Association was the a man named Alimirah. He was known as Kadda Mirah. Presently his son Mohamed is considering to be the leader of Awakala. While the grand son of Yayo Hamadu is the Deputy.

Alwan Mohamed was known as selfless and proud Wasa man who always put the interest of Afar people before his own. He died in 1973 in Dessie Hospital of natural causes.

Alwan Yayo was also a well known personality in Awsa. He was in charge of Agricultural development in Awsa and played a great role in modernizing Aysaita town. He was known for his honesty and frankness. He was caught by Deg Army before he could escape with other Afar Official to Djibouti.

In the Derg prison he was subjected to ruthlessly tormented. Finaly he was lucky enough to escape to Djibouti from where he went to Saudia Arabia. Alwan Yayo was one of the Awsa Afars that made the people of Awsa proud in his time. He survived the Derg rampage. He saw that the ignominious exit of the monster called Mangistu and fall of the Derg government. Unfortunately the Derg incarceration left deteriorating mark on his health and he died in February 1974 in Addis Ababa. Alwan Alimirah died of natural causes before the coming of Deeg while Alwan Aydahis and Alwan Abdulkader are still living in Aysaita.

Sultan Hanafare Alimirah

Hanfare Alimirah has succeeded his late father, the respected Sultan Alimirah Hanfare as Sultan of Afar people or Amoyta in Awsa. The new sultan was selected by the late sultan's children, their family members and afar elders who attended the meeting that was held in Djibouti. Sultan Hanfare Alimirah expressed their gratitude and appreciation to the president of Djibouti, Ismael Omar Guille, and the Prime Minister Delaita Mohammed Delaita, and the government and brotherly people of Djibouti for their hospitality and everything else that they have done for them. Hanfare Alimirah and his brothers thanked Prime Minister Meles Zenawi for facilitating the change that is occurring in the Afar region after passing the last sultan. The last sultan fathered many children and many of them have passed away, but there are 22 remaining, 11 male 11 female, who also have fathered many grand and great grand children for the late Sultan. A year ago when new Sultan Hanfare saw his late fathers deteriorating health, he called a meeting of all his brothers and sisters and their children to meet his residence in Jeddah, Saudi Arabia. At this meeting they discussed the matter of succession to the throne of Sultan. After the passing of the great sultan on April 9th 2011, Hanfare, again called his brothers to meet him in Djibouti to continue the matter that was at hand in the previous meeting that occurred in Jeddah. The situation did not allow all of them to meet but his brothers Ahmed Alimirah, Habib Alimirah, Osman Alimirah, and Omar Alimirah attended the meeting. After a discussion that 7 days, on May 17th 2011, the brothers and other family members and afar elders came to unanimous decision to select Hanfare Alimireah as the successor of the late Sultan Alimirah Hanfare. Ahmed Alimirah was selected as heir apparent and Habib Alimirah as coordinator. The coronation date for the new sultan is around mid-September and will be held in Aysaita, the sultanates capital in Awsa.

The New Sultan, Hanfare Alimirah

Hanfare was born in Aysaita, the capital of the sultanate, from mother Mariam Ali Omar and father Sultan Alimirah Hanfare. The late Sultan named Hnfare after his own father. As a boy, Hanfare attended school in Aysaita, later on attending Haile Selassie Secondary School in Addis Ababa. He later on continued his studies in Cairo, Egypt. In the 70s, he attended The American University in Washington, D.C. While growing up in Aysaita, he was assisting his father in anything and everything he could assist with. Hanfare has distinguished himself amongst the Afar people and many Afars consider him their hero. That is why hi s succession following his father is popularly welcomed by Afar people everywhere. During the long struggle against the Derg regime, Hanfare was leader of the Afar resistance by joining his men in the fields against the tyrant. After in inevitable fall of the Derg, Hanfare joined EPRDF leadership and entered Addis Ababa with Prime Minister Meles Zenawi. After many ups and downs, Hanfare became ambassador of Ethiopia to the State of Kuwait. Upon becoming ambassador, some difficulties with the Ethiopian government arose and he resigned his position.

Today the need for Sultan's strength and resilience has come up again as the people need him more than ever. Being the man he is, for the Afar people, Hanfare accepted the burden and responsibility that lies upon the Sultan. People's expectations of him are very high. For those of us who are close to

Hanfare, we know that he will live up to the expectations of the people and go beyond that of which is expected. Our confidence in him is high as ever and we hope and wish that he will overcome those enormous obstacles. To do so, he needs our help to help all the Afar people. In fact, the help of all of Ethiopia and the Horn of Africa. let us all come together to join hands to support him for the best future of the AFARS around the world.

AFAR News Toronto

A Newsletter connecting AFAR Community of North America

Vol. 02 Issue - 02   Publisher - Editor : Kadafo Hanfare   April 2012

This issue is dedicated

In memory of
a great Humanatarian

Professor Georges Clovis Savard
1921 - 2012

On March 27th, 2012, The Afar people lost a great crusader for the rights of Afars and a wonderful friend. Professor Georges Clovis Savard passed away at the age of 90 in Quebec City, QC, Canada. He lived in Ethiopia for 20+ years and spent 5 of those years in the Afar Region. He touched many hearts through his voyages through Aysaita, Kalabtale, and many other Afar cities. He came to know and befriend historic Afar figures such as the late Sultan Alimirah Hanfare and the late Fitawrare Yayo Hamadu. I have been fortunate enough to have had my life impacted by this great man. He took me as a young child and offered me a job as an interpreter thus giving me a chance so few ever have to observe and learn from this great pioneer. He will be dearly missed and on behalf of Sultan Hanfare Alimirah, Afar News Toronto, and Afar people everywhere, we would like to extend our whole hearted condolences to his son Arthur Savard and his daughter Mary Savard and his many friends and family members. *May his gentle soul rest in peace.*

Kadafo Mohammed Hanfare
Editor and Publisher
AFAR NEWS TORONTO

In this issue

À : Le Soleil CONTRAT : #12-0403
DE : Caron Catherine
Avis de décès pour Georges Clovis Savard
Parution pour le jeudi 29 mars et vendredi 30 mars
Responsable : Mary Curtin Savard, 3609, rue Chrétien, Wendover. K0A 3K0 téléphone : 613 405-0550

TEXTE
Georges Clovis Savard
1921 - 2012

Dr. Georges Clovis Savard né le 18 septembre 1921, époux de feu Mary Mann Wallmeyer Curtin-Savard, est décédé le 27 mars à Québec à l'âge de 90 ans.

Il laisse dans le deuil ses deux enfants, Arthur et Mary Anastasia ainsi que leurs conjoints Liliane et Alan, ses six petits-enfants, son neveu Pascal, ses nièces Louise, Johanne et Chantal, de nombreux cousins et amis.

Après une jeunesse passée à Québec, il devint Jésuite et œuvra en Éthiopie de 1947 à 1971. Il enseignait l'anglais à l'école primaire Taf Ari Makonnen, la géographie au Collège secondaire Haile Sellassie, puis l'ethnologie et les cultures éthiopiennes à l'université d'Addis Ababa.

Il a concentré sa recherche anthropologique sur les Afars, peuplade de pasteurs vivant dans la région de la mer Rouge. De retour au pays, il se sentit profondément attiré par une vie affective. Il quitta les Jésuites, se maria, et adopta les deux enfants de sa femme Mary (Arthur et Mary Anastasia) qui avaient perdu leur père. À Québec, il fut au service du Conseil des affaires sociales et de la famille. Son souci pour le bien-être des familles l'a amené à fonder avec des travailleurs sociaux ProSys inc. une entreprise offrant une approche adaptée pour aider rapidement les familles en difficultés. Il est cofondateur de la Maison de la famille à Ste Foy et récipiendaire du prix Mercure pour sa collaboration professionnelle à l'élaboration des politiques familiales du Québec.

Félicitations et remerciements à la résidence Ste-Brigitte pour les soins exceptionnels prodigués. Nous retiendrons de notre très cher Georges Clovis son inlassable souci pour le bien-être des autres. Qu'il repose maintenant en paix.

La famille recevra les condoléances, en présence du corps, à la
Coopérative funéraire des Deux Rives
Centre funéraire du Plateau
693, avenue Nérée-Tremblay, Québec G1N 4R8
Informations : 418 688-2411   Envoi d'un message de sympathie
Télécopieur : 418 688-2414
residence@coopfuneraire2rives.com

le vendredi 30 mars 2012, de 19h à 22h. Le service religieux sera célébré le samedi 31 mars 2012 à 14h en l'église Sts-Martyrs-Canadiens (735, rue Père-Marquette (coin rue des Braves), Québec). L'inhumation se fera à une date ultérieure au cimetière Belmont.

Vos témoignages de sympathie peuvent se traduire par un don aux Jésuites, téléphone : 514-387-2541, à la Société des Missions-Étrangères, téléphone : 450-667-4190, site web : www.smelaval.org ou au peuple Afar, site web : www.cangoafar.ca. Des formulaires seront disponibles sur place.

Coopérative funéraire des Deux Rives
Siège social, 280, 8e Rue
Québec (Québec) G1L 2N9
téléphone : 418 688-2411   télécopieur : 418 525-6971
residence@coopfuneraire2rives.com   www.coopfuneraire2rives.com

TO : Le Soleil CONTRACT : #12-0403
FROM : Caron Catherine
Death notice for Georges Clovis Savard
To be published on Thursday March 29th and Friday March 30th
Person in charge: Mary Curtin Savard, 3609, rue Chrétien, Wendover, K0A 3K0 Phone : 613 405-0550

TEXT

Georges Clovis Savard
1921 - 2012

Dr. Georges Clovis Savard, born on September 18th, 1921, husband of the late Mary Mann Wallmeyer Curtin-Savard, passed away at the age of 90 on March 27th in Quebec City.

He is survived by his two deeply grieved children, Arthur and Mary Anastasia, as well as by their spouses Liliane and Alan, his six grandchildren, his nephew Pascal, his nieces Louise, Johanne and Chantal, and also many cousins and friends.

After spending his youth in Quebec City, Georges Clovis became a Jesuit and worked in Ethiopia from 1947 to 1971. He taught English at Tafari Makonnen Grade School, Geography at Haile Sellassie Secondary School, and then Ethnology and Ethiopian cultures at the University of Addis Ababa.

He focused his anthropological research on the Afars, a population of shepherds living in the region bordering the Red Sea. When he returned home, he felt a deep urge to devote more attention to his own emotional life. He left the Jesuits, got married and adopted his wife Mary's two children, Arthur and Mary Anastasia, who had lost their father. He worked for the Social Affairs and Family Council in Quebec City. His concern for the welfare of families lead him to found ProSys Inc. with fellow social workers, a company whose aim was to help families in need by using an efficient and flexible approach. He was the co-founder of the Maison de la Famille in Sainte-Foy, and was awarded the Mercure prize for his professional involvement in the development of Quebec's family policies.

We would like to thank and congratulate the staff of the Sainte-Brigitte residence for the outstanding care they provided. We will always remember our dearest Georges Clovis for his relentless concern for the well-being of others. May he rest in peace now and for ever.

The family will receive condolences in presence of the body at

Coopérative funéraire des Deux Rives
Centre funéraire du Plateau
693, avenue Nérée-Tremblay, Québec G1N 4R8
Information : 418 688-2411
To send a sympathy message: Fax : 418 688-2414
residence@coopfuneraire2rives.com

on Friday, March, 30th 2012, from 7pm to 10 pm. The religious service will be held on Saturday, March 31st, at 2 pm at the Église Saints Martyrs Canadiens (735, rue Père-Marquette (corner of rue des Braves, Québec City). The burial will take place at a later date at the Belmont Cemetery.

Your testimonials of sympathy can take the form of a donation to the Jesuits, phone: 514-387-2541, to the Foreign Mission Society, phone: 450-667-4190, Website: http://www.smelaval.org/en/ or to the Afar people, Website: http://www.cangoafar.ca. Donation forms will be available on site.

Coopérative funéraire des Deux Rives
Head Office: 280, 8e rue, Québec City (Québec) G1L 2N9
phone : 418 688-2411   fax : 418 525-6971
residence@coopfuneraire2rives.com   www.coopfuneraire2rives.com

Ca me ferait du bien de vous dire que j'ai de la peine suite au décès de mon père Georges, que d'autres appellent Clovis.

Georges était mon père adoptif. Il a rencontré ma mère Mary, récemment devenue veuve, en 1971 à New York. En 1973 il nous amena tous à Québec, épousa Mary, et adopta ma soeur et moi. C'est ainsi que commença ma vie avec Georges.

J'ai de la peine parce que Georges était un personne que j'appréciais énormément et je crois que tout ceux qui l'ont connu ont le meme sentiment. Il était un homme doux, très attentif aux besoins des autres. Il ne cessait de croire que tous pouvaient se parler, travailler,et vivre ensemble harmonieusement.

J'ai de la peine parce que Georges était un home exceptionnellement instruit et ouvert d'esprit. On entretenait avec lui des conversations animés, des conversations qui nous amenaient à constater qu'il y a habituellement deux côtés valides à chaque discussion et qu'il ne faut pas sauter trop vite à une conclusion.

J'ai de la peine parce que Georges était un homme charitable, ayant renoncé à avoir ses propres enfants pour investir dans les deux qu'il avait adoptés. Avant son marriage avec Mary, il lui a dit qu'elle était la plus merveilleuse femme du monde parce que, en plus d'être belle et intélligente, elle venait en supplement avec deux adorable enfants.

J'ai de la peine parce que Georges était un guide pour la jeunesse. Lorsque nous étions petits, il passait des heures chaque soir avec ma soeur et moi pour nous aider à apprendre le français. Et avec les Jésuites, il fut professeur pour des centaines d'élèves en Éthiopie, en plus d'être leur entraineur de gymnastique.

J'ai de la peine parce que Georges était un aventurier, ayant voyage dans plus de 40 pays au cours de sa vie. Même à l'âge de 80 ans, il est venu me voir en Californie et a fait sa dernière sortie de vélo parmis les orangers avec ma femme.

J'ai de la peine parce que Georges était simple et facile à plaire. Il gardait le sourire et l'optimisme dans toutes les circonstances de la vie.

Et finalement, j'ai de la peine parce que Georges est mon père depuis 40 ans, et son depart me laisse un vide.

Lorsqu'une personne chère nous quitte, elle nous manque. Et plus la personne qui a quitté nous est chère, plus cette personne nous manque.

Je vous dirais par contre, que Georges n'aurait pas voulu que nous soyions triste pour trop longtemps. Comme j'ai mentionné, Georges voyait le positif dans tout. Lorsqu'il était prêtre en devenir, un de ses exercices fut de marcher avec ses confrères sur le trajet Montréal-Québec. Sur le chemin les jeunes hommes eurent soif, et arrêtèrent dans un presbytère pour demander à boire. La dame qui ouvrit la porte n'avait que du lait tiède à leur offrir et malheureusement ce lait avait commencé à surir. Pendant que ses amis hésitaient, Georges
en but une grande quantité et prononça: 'Merci madame pour ce bon lait, et vous avez donc bien eu une bonne idée de mettre un peu de citron dedans'.

Dans ce bel esprit de confiance et de simplicité, je vous invite à chanter avec moi une chanson que Georges aimait beaucoup.

Pack up your troubles in your old kit-bag,
And smile, smile, smile,
While you've a Lucifer to light your fag,
Smile, boys, that's the style.
What's the use of worrying?
It never was worthwhile, so
Pack up your troubles in your old kit-bag,
And smile, smile, smile.

Merci Papa, merci Georges Clovis, tu as réellement fait une difference dans ma vie et dans la vie de bien d'autres per-

4

I would like to tell you how much I grieve over the death of my father Georges, also known as Clovis.

Georges was my adoptive father. He met my mother, Mary, in New York in 1971, shortly after my father's death. In 1973, he took us all to Quebec City, married Mary and adopted my sister and me. That is how my life with Georges began.

I grieve because *I liked Georges a lot, and I believe that all those who have known him feel the same.* He was a sweet man, extremely mindful of the needs of others. He never stopped believing that all people could talk to one another, work and live together in harmony.

I grieve because Georges was *an exceptionally learned and open-minded person.* We would have lively conversations with him, which lead us to realise that there are usually two valid sides to every story and that one should not rush to conclusions.

I grieve because Georges was *a charitable man* who had given up having his own children in order to devote himself to the two he had adopted. Before his wedding to Mary, he told her that she was the most wonderful woman in the world because, in addition to being beautiful and smart, she also came with two adorable children.

I grieve because Georges was *a guide to the youth.* When we were little, he would spend hours every night helping me and my sister learn French. With the Jesuits, he taught hundreds of students in Ethiopia, in addition to being their phys-ed teacher.

I grieve because Georges was *an adventurer* who had travelled to more than 40 countries throughout his life. Even at the age of 80, he came to visit me in California and went on his last cycling trip in an orange grove with my wife.

I grieve because Georges was *simple and easy-going.* He always kept his smile and remained optimistic, no matter what.

And finally, I grieve because Georges was *my father for 40 years*, and his loss leaves me off-balance. When a close one departs, we miss them. And the closer that person is to us, the more we miss them.

However, let me tell you this: Georges would not have wanted us to be sad for too long. As I said, Georges could see the bright side of life. When he was training to become a priest, he once walked all the way from Montreal to Quebec City with his fellow priests-to-be as part of his exercise routine. Along the way, the young men got thirsty and made a break at a presbytery to ask for something to drink. The lady who opened the door only had warm milk to give them, and unfortunately, it had started to go off. While his friends were debating whether they should have it, Georges drank a big mouthful and said: "Thank you, Madam, for this delicious milk - what a great idea you had to add a little lemon juice in it!"

In this beautiful spirit of trust and simplicity, please sing along with me a song that Georges liked a lot.

Pack up your troubles in your old kit-bag,
And smile, smile, smile,
While you've a Lucifer to light your fag,
Smile, boys, that's the style.
What's the use of worrying?
It never was worth while, so
Pack up your troubles in your old kit-bag,
And smile, smile, smile.

Thank you Dad, thank you Georges Clovis, you really made a difference in my life, as well as in that of many other people.

The Peoples of Ethiopia

by George Clovis Savard

The purpose of this article is two-fold. First, to schematize our present knowledge of the prehistory of Ethiopia.[1] That is admittedly only a tentative effort because even though Ethiopia can boast to be the only country in East Africa with a "history", its prehistory is still very little known. Much of our knowledge of the Upper Paleolithic, the Mesolithic and the Neolithic in Ethiopia is derived from the study of the sites and movements of prehistoric populations in the territories adjacent to Ethiopia. Often we can only surmise by inference what may have happened and -occasionally must have happened in Ethiopia. It should be clear then that many of the statements that follow must be checked by archeologists, linguists and ethnologists who will have the privilege to work in Ethiopia. At the present moment, a tentative synthesis is valuable only if it helps research to orient itself better.[2] In the second part of this article an attempt will be made to describe briefly some of the most significant cultural traits that can be observed in various ethnic groups of today.

1. TIME PERSPECTIVES

In 1928, Teilhard de Chardin discovered Porcupine Cave, a few miles south of Diredawa. Four years later the cave, excavated by P. Wernert, was yielding the only well-identified prehistoric human remains found in Ethiopia. They consist of the right part of a mandible with molars and premolars. No one, it seems, doubts that this is a human jaw although it shows "archaic" traits: massive bones, absence of chin, very large teeth, etc.

What did the possessor of the jaw look like? Perhaps like the Neanderthals, but more probably like the ancestors of the modern Hottentots. He lived some time between 10,000 and 15,000 years ago. Yet he did not belong to the first population that settled in the Horn. Stone tools discovered by Desmond Clark and Italian archeologists reveal that this part of Africa had already been inhabited for thousands of years by peoples whose cultures have been labeled *Upper*

Acheulian, the earliest culture now *in situ* and found in numerous parts of Ethiopia, *Levalloisian* for the last pluvial (Gamblian) 70,000 to 10,000 years ago, and *Still bay* for the dry post pluvial period.

The makers of these tools were not much different perhaps from the proto-Bushman found in Singa (Sudan), or from the proto-Australoid from Eyasi (Tanganyika). They were not Negroid, however, because the Negroes came to East Africa much later, e.g., after the beginning of the Neolithic, in Kenya). The most plausible hypothesis is that they were Bushmen.

During the 5th millennium B.C., agriculture was developing rapidly in West Sudan. It may have been stimulated by Egypt, but Murdock's analysis of botanical, ethnographic and linguistic data seems to indicate an independent innovation and thus we could add the invention of agriculture to the credit of one of the "purest" negro populations in Africa.

The 4th millennium B.C., very likely, saw the propagation of agriculture eastward and, in the area that concerns us, the last phases of the Hargeisan culture (in existence perhaps since the beginning of the Gamblian). The Hargeisan is a stone culture characterized by blades and similar to the Caspian cultures of Kenya and Tunisia (perhaps just a phenomenon of parallel evolution). The Hargeisan industry is clearly distinct from the industries of the " Bushmen" and, according to Bailloud, must be attributed to a different stock, a population of " Homo Sapiens ". Murdock, trying to be more explicit, describes them as Caucasoid and proto-Cushites.

In the course of time, the Wiltonian industry superseded the Hargeisan and' eventually became dominant in the totality of South and East Africa. Characterized by Micro lithic tools: lunates and thumbnail scrapers, made of obsidian, it is found in numerous sites, from Harar to Sidamo, and from Yavello, through Moggio, Debre Zeit to the Dahlak Archipelago. This industry lasted till comparatively recent times; in fact during historical times, in Djebel Djinn (Côte Française des Somalis).

The Doian industry finally appeared in the South and Centre of the Somali Plateau. A very late derivative of the Magosian, it reveals the importance of hunting, the beginnings of animal domestication and, perhaps, incipient agriculture in the site of Mersale Wells.

In Ethiopia, it is very difficult to utilize stone industries in order to determine the beginning of the Neolithic period (village farming communities). Ground stones are extremely rare, except in the southwest where Azais discovered abundant artifacts establishing the existence of Neolithic agriculturists who spread, he thought, from the Beni Shangul territory to Lake Rudolf. Decorated ceramics and even some metal implements were found in association with the stone tools. Thus the gap would be bridged between the Neolithic of the Sudan and that of Kenya.

Murdock believes that this agricultural "revolution" occurred circa 3000 B.C.: Negroes broke through the western frontier, settled in Wallega and then brought agriculture to the Plateau. The Agau, thereafter, demonstrated a remarkable spirit of inventiveness, even if they owed agriculture to the invaders. They discovered new varieties of the cultivated plants introduced by the Negroes, e.g., *durra*, but they also enabled some of the plants that grew wild, and originated a cultivation that has lasted till our day: finger millet *(dagussa), teff, enset,* cress, safflower, coffee, *kat,* kastor, etc. It appears also that the Agau domesticated the donkey and discovered how to breed mules.

About 2250 B.C. the pastoralists Beja, or their ancestors, gained much territory in Southern Sudan and acquired lands that had belonged to flourishing Negro farming communities for over 1,500 years. On the Red Sea, for centuries already, the Egyptians had been sending expeditions to the land of Punt (today the" Côte Française Somalis "), while on the highlands, the Cushites of Ethiopia had begun a diversification which separated them into three great groups: the Central Agau, the Western and the Eastern Cushites.

Towards the end of the 2nd millennium, we can assume cat the southern Cushitic population started fanning out in a great expansion movement that stopped only on the parallel of six degrees South latitude. In fact, East African archaeology reveals the presence (1000 B.C.) of a very restricted group of peoples who knew agriculture very well and who settled on the highlands (perhaps beause they enjoyed a heavier rainfall) of Uganda, Kenya and Northern Tanganyika. The population living today on, or about, these sites have been called "Hamitized Negroes" and" Nilo-Hamites ", and there some evidence (although some linguists disagree) suggesting that these populations once spoke a Cushitic language. But more significant perhaps is the fact that contemporary highland peoples (e.g., the Nandi, Meru, Hill Suk, Chagga) who occupy sites that were perhaps :led by prehistoric southern Cushites also share a certain number of traits that seem to predominate among the Cushitic populations of Ethiopia. An exhaustive inventory of traits should be taken, even at the risk of ruining this demonstration.

At the beginning of the 1st millennium B.C., the Sabeans came across the Red Sea to Ethiopia. They brought with them the arts and skills of a civilization which could boast remarkable achievements, especially perhaps in agriculture and trade. It was not long before they sailed south and reached the Horn. Murdock[3] speaks of "historical sources" saying that Himyaritic Arabs of South Arabia controlled the coastal towns of what is now the Côte Française des Somalis and British Somaliland for perhaps 10 centuries B.C. Later (about 60 AD.) we learn from the Periplus of the Erythraean Sea that the Yemeni merchants then on the coast of "Somalia" and "Kenya" were married to local women and understood the native language. But was the native population Cushitic? Archaeology points to the affirmative because traces of Negroid occupation are absent for many centuries. Other facts also seem to confirm this view: in particular the presence of phallic stones, along the coast, like those found in great numbers in Southern Ethiopia (there is even one on the Entoto, in Addis Ababa).

Perhaps during the second half of the 1st millennium B.C., Yemeni immigrant (?) converted to pre-Talmud Judaism a group of northern Cushites whose descendants we know as the Felasha. The same period of time must have witnessed the rapid rise of Axum, seemingly with very little interference, or help, from Egypt, Rome or Greece. It was an original evolution and a fairly swift one, since in the 4th and 6th centuries AD. the Axumites were able to return across the Red Sea to go and fight with their allies.

7

In the first centuries after Christ, the Yemeni began to dominate the African coast of the Indian Ocean as far south as Kilwa. They lasted until the time almost of the Portuguese, except for some 300 years (575-879 A.D.) when the "Persians" took over control and extended the trade of Arabia-Africa as far as China.

At the beginning of the second half of the 1st millennium A.D. a great migration began to take shape. The Bantu started their sensational trek to the East and, after crossing the forests of the mpygmies; they encircled Lake Victoria and ultimately reached the coast, probably during the period when the Persians were in control of the trade. Azania, the coast of southern Somalia, Kenya and Tanganyika, was then in full prosperity and, very likely, it was the Azanians, eager to exploit the rich mines of the interior, who caused the building of the complex structures of Zimbabwe and Mapungubwe (carbon date: beginning of 7th C.A.D.). Already gold and slaves were pouring in quantity out of East Africa.

Meanwhile, a population from the Nile, perhaps after having learned the art of dairying (from the Beja?) began expanding with explosive force. These Nilotes moved south, were deflected to the east by the better organized Bantu kingdoms of Uganda, and finally reached the Rift Valley in Kenya and Tanganyika. Little by little, the highland farmers who had been there for some 2,000 years found themselves surrounded by Bantu and Nilotic populations. The process of assimilation began to take place and the Cushitic peoples lost their identity more and more. Today, we can identify only a few Cushitic speaking groups, all of them separated by a distance of at least 400 miles from their Cushitic "brothers" of Ethiopia. We can name the *Burungi*, the *Goroa*, the *s* and the *Mbugu*.

At approximately the same time, a similar population explosion was probably taking place in the upper regions of the Somali Plateau. Agriculturists belonging to the stock that gave rise to the Agau, but unchanged yet by Christianity or Semitic influence, were learning (?) in their turn the techniques of pastoral life that had trickled from the north (?) or the west (?). One group rapidly branched off and started to ntove northward and settled in what is now the arid Afar (Dankali) desert. At the same time (or perhaps before) another group started moving east and south. These were the ancestors of the modern Galla (Oromo) and-it seems-they liberally dotted a considerable part of the Horn with their sites.

Finally, a third group, one with seemingly greater cultural maturity, began with the help of herds of animals to spread over the lowlands. Soon, enough of these ancestors of our contemporary Somali discovered that many peoples had preceded them into the Horn:

The Galla and the Bantu, who had already intermarried very much, and the first occupants of all, the Bushmen.4 Above all, there were always imigrants coming from Arabia or Yemen. Some of them, with the prestige given by a superior knowledge of Islam, became the ancestors (or were adopted as ancestors) of lineages that have become very numerous today.

Hundreds of years later, probably in the 13th century AD., the Galla began to feel the pressure of the Somali expansion on the coast. And, at about the same time, with the re-establishment of the Solomonian dynasty, Abyssinian influence reached the south and south-west. But because of the presence of Islamic powers also competing for these areas, this influence was felt only sporadically. It is possible that lexicostatistics will, some day, trace to this period the beginning of the Gurage languages from their Sidamo, Amharic and Harari substrata.5

In the 14th century the Somali occupied the coast of Somalia as far as the lower Sibeli, and in the 15th century they held the whole valley of the sibeli for themselves. Pushed out of the Somali territory, the Galla6 tried, soon after the defeat of Ahmed Gran, to infiltrate into Abyssinia from the South. But the Abyssinians, exhausted by war, let the Galla add conquest to conquest during a good 50 years. Some Sidamo states were conquered and became Galla states in the course of time, but other kingdoms proved so strong as to preserve their existence. (In fact, the Galla never acquired any land south of the Godjeb.) In the 20th century, it was left to Menelik to recover lands that had been long forsaken and to give Ethiopia its modern look.

MODERN ETHIOPIA IN THE MAKING

The population of Ethiopia, like that of every old nation, is a miniature world in itself with, certainly, a very remarkable wealth of cultures, or sub-cultures, all different enough from the rest of African cultures to constitute an original unit in themselves. But a unit with many faces, a unit so complex that any attempt at schematizing the facts or streamlining the conclusions can be a distortion of reality; should we stress, for instance, unity or plurality?

Sultan Hanfare Alimirah

Sultan Hanfare Alimirah

FUNDRAISING 2012

Ahmed Youssef, Prof. Magnet, Mallika, Mr. Creates & Abdi

Mr. Creates addressing the audience

Amb. Kadafo addressing the audience

Mallika addressing the audience

Prof. Magnet accepting
AFAR Citizenship certificate

Mr. Creates accepting
AFAR Citizenship certificate

Mr. Creates and Prof. Magnet

Prof. Magnet and Mallika

Mr. Creates addressing the audience

Mallika addressing the audience

Ladies dancing

The tendency nowadays is to emphasize unity, to speak of Ethiopians instead of Oromo, Amhara or Gurage. This is a healthy orientation and a well-timed shift of emphasis. At the moment when there is so much talk about Pan-Africanism, one would have to be the worst type of "reactionary" to insist on differences between Tigri, Gojjamites and Gondari. Nevertheless, if we want to speak of a population as rich in human cultures as that of Ethiopia, we must use a certain amount of classificatory devices.

One working distinction could be made between urban and rural segments of the population. In Addis Ababa, for example, ethnic or tribal affiliations matter little (how little, especially when it comes to marriages, I will let the reader decide), and certainly the Senate, the executive branches of the Government, the Ecclesiastical Hierarchy, the Army and even the U.C.AA Student Council are generally established on principles different from those of ethnic origins.

But when we come to rural populations, the degree to which ethnic affiliations have vanished varies. The feeling of being an Ethiopian first can be very great in some groups, and it could be increased in others. But there is nothing strange in that state of affairs. That should even appear normal to us when we reflect on the complex historical background of Ethiopia and we should perhaps rather marvel at the rapidity with which national consciousness is developing in Ethiopia, integrating at higher and higher levels age-old particularisms that once kept people wide apart. A whole study could be made only on the institutions that have favoured, and hindered, this growth of the Ethiopian nation.

Now if I single out some ethnic groups in Ethiopia, it will not be to stress their differences as much as to show some aspects of their contribution to the quality of the Ethiopian society as a whole. I am interested in unity, but I am also interested in variety, in as much as it is a fact, and a reality. I am interested in what we could call the various types of cultures in Ethiopia simply because they exist. I do not particularly hope to preserve any specific tradition-that is not my business -but I want to understand what Ethiopia is made of and what will likely be the substance of tomorrow's society. Many things will disappear, more or less rapidly, some of which

were probably very valuable when they were incorporated in a body of tradition; others will be preserved. On the other hand, the population of Ethiopia will not be made up only of urbanized citizens, far less of "been to's" who sometimes have dissociated themselves from their own ethnic groups. It will be composed, largely, of the descendants of the rural people of today and it seems worthwhile to consider what sort of enrichment these will bring to the population of Ethiopia as a whole. Let us then single out some areas of Ethiopian culture in which we find sections of our population ready to make various contributions, or forced to face specific problems, in the process of modernization. I shall limit myself mostly to ethnic groups that are less known, some of them also less developed than others, but all of them; capable of participating fully in the life of modern Ethiopia.

Although the Amhara and Tigri are among the best situation, it is easy to surmise, surely stands half way mutual help described by Dr. R. K. P. Pankhurst, and Endreas Eshete in the "Ethiopia Observer",[7] and by Temesgien Gobena and Asfaw Damte in the 7th and 8th issues of the "Ethnological Society Bulletin".[8] *Ekub, Idir, Dabo, Jige* and other forms of friendship societies are well known and I do not think I have to dwell on them. Let me just mention, 'however, an archaic group of the southwest, the *Ari*, who have an original form of co-operative system. There, the young men join to form labour organizations. They will work in co-operation and go from place to place offering their services in times when the demand for labour is greater.

These young workers constitute some kind of agegroup reminiscent of a system almost extinct today but one that once formed the backbone of Oromo society. It is the *Gada*. The *Gada* used to divide the whole Oromo population into five groups, let us call them A. B, C, D, E. If you were in group B, you would normally remain in it for the rest of your participation in the *Gada* and you would move with all your fellows from Group B (whether they be in Addis Ababa or any other part of Ethiopia), through five grades lasting eight years each. Let us suppose that you join the *Gada* cycle in 1960 as a member of Group A. Eight years later you would become a learning warrior, then in 1976 a warrior in service. After eight more years you would be a learning elder, i.e. from 1984 to 1992, and then from 1992 to the second millennium you would belong to the grade of the rulers. The marvelous thing about the *Gada* is that it used to cut across every possible category in the Oromo society and unite together people who could have been separated by geography, religion, political or tribal affiliations. An Oromo, for instance, in the second grade was very intimately related to any other Oromo of the same grade in the whole of Ethiopia. There were characteristics of the Gada system that would, of course, never fit into modern Ethiopia, but one wonders whether some aspects of it could not be salvaged for the benefit of the new Ethiopia, where such a solidarity is going to have a survival value.

Now let us touch on another vital point. A cultural trait is usually important only in relation to its cultural context. For instance, it is only because the people were Oromo that they pointed with their third finger. But some cultural traits may correspond to some fundamental needs in the development of civilisation, and for that reason assume an almost absolute character of necessity. I think that the capacity of the Gurage for manual work is one such case. The only people who would perhaps like to contest this point are the Gurage themselves because they are not so sure that love for manual work is really a Gurage trait. Among the Gurage there are three submerged castes, or segments of the population who are kept apart, may only marry among themselves, and even If they are called upon to perform important ritual functions, e.g. at birth or at death, are nevertheless looked down upon because of the kind of work they are doing. These three Gurage castes are, from the bottom up, the *Fuga* who make wooden chairs, tables of bamboo, doors, etc. (Fuga women make pots); second, *the Buda*, who are leatherworkers, and third the *Nafere*, poor blacksmiths who, however. enjoy a little and rather ironical compensation: their women are most beautiful even though taboo for all the other Gurage. Some other traits are so deeply rooted in a culture that they change very slowly. The Customary Law is one such area of conflict where the forces of tradition and those of innovation can battle for a long while. There are innumerable points of readjustment between traditional laws and the new civil and criminal codes, and some of the most difficult problems will doubtless arise about land ownership. One can imagine what different riddles the legislator faces when one thinks that in Tigre there are lands still owned in common by many people, in Kaffa there were no private awnings, the land being the exclusive property of the Kaffa kings, and in the deserts and semi-deserts the concept of property is often inalienably united to the idea of occupation; a piece of land that is not cultivated is yours to pasture your animals on whenever you wish, especially if you are strong. Evidently, it will not be easy for the new law to supersede the old one, but this will come about eventually, and it will ultimately become clear that the new state of things is as well adapted and efficient as the former one.

---

[1] Ethiopia" Is used here to designate the territory comprised within the boundaries of contemporary Ethiopia and Eritrea. "Abyssinia" is reserved for the 'Old kingdom of the Central Highlands.

[2] [3] George Murdoch's **Africa: Its People and their Cultural History** was largely relied upon in this first part.

[4] This process. that we could call the "pastoralization" of farmers, is still happening nowadays. The members of the Frobenius Institute who visited the southwest, less than 10 yeas ago, claim that the Tsamako. who live north of Lake Stefanie, are actually in the process of becoming cattldee breers and lowland people. In this way they are breaking a long tradition because they used to practice agriculture on the highlands, exactly what their neighbours have been doing, and are still doing to this day.

[5] It is more Uk,ely, however, that the origins 'Of the Gm'age and the Harari could be traced back to a minor i nvasion from south Arabia during the Axumite ,period, perhaps ,between the 5th and the 7th Centuries A.D.

[6] In the 19th Century they were pushed back further to the River Tana in Kenya.

[7] Ethiopia Observer, Vol. II, No. 211, December, 1958. [8] University College of Addis Ahaba: Ethnological Society Bulletin No.7, December, 1957; Bulletin NO.8, July, 1958.

SELECTED BIBLIOGRAPHY

BAILLOUD, Gerard: "La Prehistoire de l'Ethiopie," in "Cahiers de l'Afrique et l'Asie," V.l5-43, 1959.

CLARK, J. Desmond: "The Prehistoric Cultures of the Horn of Africa," Cambridge, 1954.

COLE. Sonia: "The Prehistory of East Africa," Penguin Books Ltd., 1954.

MURDOCK, George P.: "Africa: Its Peoples and Their Cultural History." McGraw-Hill Book Co. Inc., 1959.

Ethnographic Survey of Africa, edited by Daryll Forde, International African Institute, London.

CERULLI, Ernesta: "The Peoples of South-West Ethiopia and its Borderland," 1956.

HUNTINGFORD, G. W. B.: "The Galla of Ethiopia," 1955.

LEWIS, I. M.: "Peoples of the Horn of Africa," 1955.

Reprinted from Ethiopia Observer, Vol. V, No.3, 1961

Joe Magnet: *the accidental statesman*

In an improbable sequence of events, an Ottawa law Prof has taken on the constitutional cause of the Afar people in Africa.

by **Brad Mackay**

April 2, 2012

It's a sweltering October day in Logia, a remote desert town in Northern Ethiopia, and Joe Magnet is patiently sitting - and sweating - in a room packed with 150 chanting, self-styled freedom fighters. The men belong to the Red Sea Afar Democratic Organization, or RSADO, a paramilitary group supported by the Ethiopian government whose job it is to defend the rights and well-being of the Afar, a nomadic indigenous tribe that has existed in the Horn of Africa for more than 2,000 years.

On most days this involves patrolling the contentious border between Ethiopia and Eritrea or protecting against attacks by Al-Shabaab, the notorious Islamist organization that calls nearby Somalia home. But today they're sitting behind children's desks inside this scrubby one-room schoolhouse, whose yellow walls are plastered with homemade political posters and RSADO banners. Joe Magnet, a member of the University of Ottawa's law faculty, is front and centre, taking long slugs from a bottle of water as men with cameras and camcorders jostle for space around him in the 42 C heat.

Though he looks uncomfortable, he's not here against his will. In fact he's a guest of honour. That's because for the past 18 months Professor Magnet has been serving as legal counsel to the Afar, advising them on a series of constitutional and human rights issues. *A well-known authority on constitutional law in Canada*, he's chosen up until now not to publicly discuss his pro-bono work with the Afar back home. His clients, on the other hand, have been decidedly less circumspect.

After his first visit to this vast arid lowland region in 2010, the Afar wrote countless news stories about Professor Magnet, posted more than a half-dozen videos of him on YouTube, and the Red Sea Afar changed their name to better reflect his ideas. They even gave him his own tribal name, "Madab-abba," which translates into "Father of the Constitution."

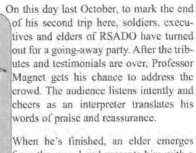

Professor Joe Magnet.
Photo by DanielEhrenworth.

On this day last October, to mark the end of his second trip here, soldiers, executives and elders of RSADO have turned out for a going-away party. After the tributes and testimonials are over, Professor Magnet gets his chance to address the crowd. The audience listens intently and cheers as an interpreter translates his words of praise and reassurance.

When he's finished, an elder emerges from the crowd and presents him with a gold-framed picture of the group's logo. Moved by the humble and heart-felt keepsake, Professor Magnet hoists the picture over his head in an impulsive gesture of joy and triumph. The men are still cheering when he exits the building with a broad grin stretching across his face.

A few minutes later in the open-air of the savannah, Madab-abba pauses in front of an idling Land Cruiser and contemplates the bizarre scenario that just played out. "What the hell am I doing here?" he blurts out. "I mean, who the fuck do I think I am? The Jewish Che Guevera?"

It's a good question, and typical coming from this man, who possesses a deeply arch view of the world. After all, here he was: a 65-year-old vegetarian Jew working for meat-raising Muslims in one of the hottest and most perilous places on earth. His close friend, Ottawa lawyer Lawrence Greenspon, would call this one of Professor Magnet's "Woody Allen moments"– a time when he is keenly aware of the human comedy and the role he plays in it.

For instance, Professor Magnet would be the first to admit it that he makes an unlikely statesman for these tenacious, proud people. Until a few years ago, he had no clue who the Afar even were. He first heard of them in 2008, after a chance encounter with Warren Creates at a neighbour's Christmas party. A well-known immigration lawyer and old acquaintance, Mr. Creates brought him up to speed on non-profit work he was

15

doing with a little-known Ethiopian tribe of pastoralists. The story continued at lunch a few weeks later, when Mr. Creates enthused about Can-Go Afar, the charity he had founded that was building water filters, funding schools, establishing scholarships and delivering aid to Afar refugees (who have been subject to persecution inside Eritrea ever since the country became independent from Ethiopia in 1991). Photos were shown, stories were told, and before long the lunch had transformed into a recruiting drive.

"It sounded very grand and adventurous," Professor Magnet said recently in his Ottawa home, "but I wasn't really sure what he wanted from me. Plus, I had real security concerns because I had a young daughter at the time, so I wasn't too sure about the whole thing." Besides, Professor Magnet was at a stage in his life where he says he "wasn't looking to pad out my resumé."

As that resumé will attest, over the past 35 years Joe Magnet's name has become synonymous with minority rights and constitutional law in Canada. The first of his 18 books, Constitutional Law of Canada, originally published nearly three decades ago, is currently in its ninth edition and remains one of the definitive textbooks on the subject.

Over the years, in addition to his work as a teacher and scholar, he has served as counsel in more than 200 constitutional cases in Ontario, Quebec, Manitoba and the Supreme Court of Canada. These included high-profile cases involving religious minorities, women's groups and francophone minorities, the last a landmark case in Manitoba that earned him hate mail and death threats.
Over the past two decades, most of his casework has shifted towards Aboriginal populations; in 1999 he became general counsel to the Congress of Aboriginal Peoples and he is currently involved in three major cases for First Nations, one an important treaty case in Ontario that is ongoing.

"I knew he was respected in Aboriginal law circles in Canada," Mr. Creates says, "and these people, the Afar, were likely the original Aboriginal people." Despite some initial reluctance, the more Professor Magnet researched the Afar, the more engaged he became.

Where the Afar reside: *The nomadic Afar people live in three countries, with the majority (1.3 million to 2 million) in Ethiopia. Within Ethiopia, most reside in the Afar Region, a federated ethnic state.*

The Afar can be found across the Horn of Africa, but the vast majority (about 1.25 million) reside in Ethiopia's Danakil region, a difficult expanse of desert and sub-savannah. Despite the Afar's low profile outside Ethiopia, they boast a rich pedigree that stretches back to Old Testament times - and beyond, if ethnographers are correct. "Afar" literally means "people" and linguists have posited that it may have influenced the naming of Africa itself. What's more, Lucy, a 3.2-million-year-old hominid believed to be Earth's first evidence of human life, was discovered in Ethiopia's Danakil Depression, the Afar's ancestral land, in a region that has since been dubbed the Cradle of Humanity.

The area also happens to be one of the hottest places on earth, with temperatures that can crest above 50 C in the summer, making their way of life - which involves travelling the desert on foot with goats, sheep or cattle in tow - especially grueling. Yet despite hard lives and a reputation for ferociousness, those who have met the Afar in person (such as Mr. Creates) speak of the Afar's kindness, generosity and humility.

It was more than enough to hook Professor Magnet. According to Mr. Creates, within a couple of months the Afar cause had "burrowed its way into his head and his heart."

16

In July 2010 the pair journeyed to Samara, the capital of the Afar state, a far-flung city on an elevated plain more than 600 km north of Addis Ababa.

"I had very low expectations of the trip," says Professor Magnet. "I was asked to come along, but I wasn't sure why."

He broke bread with the president of the Afar Region and delivered a speech praising multi-nation federalism, a constitutional framework of which he believes Canada is a shining example. The turning point came when a group of Afar elders asked to meet with him. The meeting took place at night under the stars, with Professor Magnet and a few others sitting at a long table across from 200 or so elders and clan leaders.

"We were placed at the head of this big table and we didn't quite understand why, so we just sat there, talking and joking," he recalls. "We were waiting for something to happen, without realising that we were what was happening.

"Then one of the elders spoke up and said, 'I'm not an educated man, I don't know how to read and write, but we don't feel properly respected here. We don't really like what we're seeing."

Professor Magnet listened intently to what the man was saying, which included stories of human rights abuses in Eritrea and camps that were overflowing with Afar refugees.

"There have been several moments in the enormity and the heat of the moment that Joe realised the importance of his role in things," observes Mr. Creates, "and that was definitely one of them."

When the man was done talking, Professor Magnet said, "You might not know how to read or write, but it is very clear from the respect that everybody holds of you that you are a very wise man. I can see that myself, and I want to tell you that I've come here to help you with your problems. And I will spare no effort to do that." "It became clear to me then," he recalls, "that I had been thrust into the centre of this."

Since that moment, Professor Magnet has devoted hundreds of hours to the Afar cause. He has met with senior Ethiopian government officials and Canada's

Foreign Affairs department (to debrief them on his activities in the country), and has delivered food and clothing to refugee camps. He's also drafted two human rights complaints on behalf of the Afar, one for the

Professor Magnet visits a UN refugee camp in Asayita, Ethiopia, during his first trip to the country in July 2010. The camp shelters members of the Afar who fled neighbouring Eritrea. Photo courtesy of Warren Creates.

United Nations Human Rights Council, the other for the UN Special Rapporteur on Indigenous Peoples, ensuring they were officially recognized as indigenous people.

Since that moment, Professor Magnet has devoted hundreds of hours to the Afar cause. He has met with senior Ethiopian government officials and Canada's Foreign Affairs department (to debrief them on his activities in the country), and has delivered food and clothing to refugee camps. He's also drafted two human rights complaints on behalf of the Afar, one for the United Nations Human Rights Council, the other for the UN Special Rapporteur on Indigenous Peoples, ensuring they were officially recognized as indigenous people.

"This Afar nationality is intensely proud. It's joined by a language, by a religion, by a territory and by a way of life - a tough life that few outsiders ever see. And it will probably be undergoing a rapid transformation very soon," Professor Magnet says. "That's tremendously intellectually interesting as an example of what you find in federations around the world that are wracked by identity politics. So, I was looking at it through that lens, and I got very interested."
But his most significant contribution may be the Samara Declaration, a document that condemns the "ongoing killings, persecution, torture, repression,

expulsion, and other unlawful mistreatment" of the Afar by the Eritrean forces, calls for international action to stop "atrocities" and, perhaps most controversially, lays out a multi-ethnic constitutional framework for Eritrea, which he considers a failed state.

In his eyes, the 21-year-old country of Eritrea is a brutal dictatorship that is ripe for an Arab Spring-styled democratic uprising. "If Cuba is a prison," he says, "then Eritrea is a torture chamber."

He is not alone in this appraisal. Reporters Without Borders has ranked Eritrea at the bottom of its annual Press Freedom Index for five years in a row (below China and North Korea), the CIA has accused it of being a hotbed for human trafficking, and the UN has placed sanctions on the country - twice - for a host of alleged offences which include supplying money and weapons to Al-Shabaab.

These are among the reasons that the Red Sea Afar Democratic Organization was formed. As one of the groups that fought for Eritrean independence alongside then-rebel leader (and now Eritrean president) Isaias Afewerki, RSADO maintains that the Afar were never granted the rights and freedoms they were promised before the revolution. They believe that under the current regime they are subject to bigotry, discrimination and persecution, including imprisonment, torture and death.

Until recently the bulk of RSADO's efforts at regime change have been martial in nature. Press releases boast about armed incursions into Eritrea and list the number of enemy soldiers that have been killed or captured.

An avowed humanist, Professor Magnet looks forward to a day when the Afar minority can live inside Eritrea without fear - and does not advocate armed conflict as a means to that end. His ideas about constitutional reform as a tool seem to have had an influence on the organization's world view. While they haven't quite given up their trusty Kalashnikovs, they have embraced his perspective, and even some of his language. The RSADO website quotes John A. MacDonald's concept of federalism and uses part of the Samara Declaration - "The right to self-determination up to secession" - as its motto (an assertion not uniformly supported in the Horn of Africa, or even among the Afar themselves).

Professor Magnet's endgame here is to try to export Canada's successful brand of multi-ethnic federalism as a solution to the problems faced by the Afar inside Eritrea.

"It's the only solution that has been known to work in the experience of world history for states like this," he explains. "The Canadian example was very pregnant. I told people that had we not made the necessary accommodations in Canada, we probably would not have the state we now have. It probably would have fractured and failed in the 1980s. We made very difficult adjustments, but it is working. The benefits are very rich: people are free, enabled and liberated. So what do you want to happen for you?"

As of this February, the academic's work had expanded to include a proposed documentary that would capture the life of the Afar at this critical juncture in their history. Even the recent news that a group of tourists had been attacked, and five killed, by unknown gunmen near Erta Ale was not enough to make him change his plans.

"What drives him is his love of people," says Mr. Greenspon. "He doesn't distinguish colour or creed or race or religion. And I think what he loves, even more than people, is his ability to make their lives better in some small way. He gets a real high from being able to do that - and it's something I can certainly understand." His work has even garnered official approval from the Ethiopian government. Michael Tobias Babisso, consul general at the Ethiopian Consulate in Canada, calls Professor Magnet "a respected scholar, an accomplished lawyer and a substantial human being," and says, "His work over the past few years has significantly benefited the Afar People as well as Ethiopia more generally. Both the Ethiopian federal government and the state government of Afar fully endorse his work. We thank him for his truly impressive commitment. We honour 'Professor Joe' and encourage him to continue."

The Core of Human Rights violation Areas in Afar Region of Ethiopia

AHRO | April 7, 2012

Afar Human Rights organization (AHRO) repeatedly discloses about human rights violations in Afar region, which is blocked for internal and external media. Many atrocities and human rights abuses have been committed against the Afar civilians in the region, where most cases remain unrevealed and unreported.

Tourists from the group who were attacked in Ethiopia's northern Afar region arrive in Addis Ababa on January 18. The rebel attack received wide international coverage but not the government atrocities that continue to beset the Afar people (AFP Photo/Jenny Vaughan) Although the recent killing and abduction of foreign tourists near Erta Ale, put the Afar Region in focus for international media, the government retaliation and harassment on local civilian population in Zone 2 has gained little attention. There is an ongoing mass imprisonment in Zone 2 and many who are allegedly accused of sympathizing with Afar oppositions have lost their jobs.

The huge sugarcane plantations along the Awash Valley supported by two huge Dams (Kassam-Kabana and Tandaho) continue to displace the pastoralist community en mass from their homes. These huge multinational investments are guarded by TPLF-led government army. Displacement for plantation left thousands of innocent civilians without pasture land, water spots and curtailed livestock movement. The Sugarcane plantations are regularly showered by prohibited pesticides that are directly dumped into the Awash river that is the lifeline of the majority of Afar people. This irresponsible chemical utilization has shown to have both short- and long-term adverse effects on the health of the population. The water canals, bushes, and pastures are contaminated causing an environmental disaster the powerfully affects the ecosystem of the Awash Valley. As recent as this week a huge chemical dumping on the main Awash River made it impossible to approach the River, and those who are dependent on the river for drinking water are now without access to water. Due to this humans and livestock are getting sick from an unidentified disease and there is no medical supply to alleviate the current disaster. Afar Human rights Organization has vowed its concern on this issue already in 2007. (http://www.sudantribune.com/Ethiopian-Govt-endangers-Afar,22705.)

Recently the displaced local communities of Doho went to Addis Ababa to file the case to the prime minister's office, but returned empty handed. Nevertheless, anyone who questions the intention of the government projects in any form is regarded as an opposition sympathizer and is subject to severe punishment without due process. About five days ago, there was a mass arrest that included pregnant women, the elderly and children in Aysaita and Dubti. The reason was that these people refused and opposed land grabbing in the localities of Dubtie and Aysaita. Other innocent civilians have been taken either to unknown prisons. Some are transported to prisons far way from their home. Still others are kept on bail of thousands of Birr which pastoralist families cannot afford and are forced to house arrest on irregular bases.

Therefore we call on:
1) Ethiopian Human Rights Commission, The Red Cross and the Amnesty International to visit unjustly impris oned civilian in Abaala, Aysaita and Adebtoli towns as soon as possible.
2) International community to investigate the atrocities committed in Afar Region along the Awash Valley and other TPLF-affiliated investment areas;
3) Investigate and help the displaced pastoralist civilians;
4) Investigate the magnitude of environmental disaster and the use of chemicals the Awash Valley.
For further information please contact: ahro2006@hotmail.com